MANAGING STRESS

MANAGING STRESS
A CREATIVE JOURNAL

SECOND EDITION

Brian Luke Seaward, Ph.D.
Center for Human Caring
University of Colorado, Denver

JONES AND BARTLETT PUBLISHERS
Sudbury, Massachusetts

Boston   London   Singapore

Editorial, Sales and Customer Service Offices
Jones and Bartlett Publishers
40 Tall Pine Drive
Sudbury, MA 01776
800-832-0034
508-443-5000
Info@jbpub.co
http://www.jbpub.com

Jones and Bartlett Publishers International
Barb House, Barb Mews
London W6 7PA
UK

Library of Congress Cataloging-in-Publication Data

Seaward, Brian Luke
    Managing Stress : a creative journal / Brian Luke Seaward. — 2nd ed.
        p. cm.
    Includes bibliographical references.
    ISBN 0-7637-0281-1 (alk. paper)
    1. Stress management. 2. Diaries—Therapeutic use. 3. Diaries—
Authorship. I. Title.
    RA785.S433 1996
    155.9'042—dc21
                                                                96-39265
                                                                    CIP

Credits: pp. ix, 14, 22, 112, 116, Rafael Millán; pp. xvii, 156, Gail Seaward Wall; pp. xix, 54, Sam Campagna; pp. 1 *(Three Bears Heads)*, 10 *(Sea Otter)*, and 150 *(Monarch Butterfly)*, Diana Dee Tyler, © 1981, reprinted with permission; pp. 2, 32, 44, 58, 78, 130, 136, Roger Navis; p. 6, © 1984, ZIGGY and Friends, Inc., distributed by Universal Press Syndicate, reprinted with permission, all rights reserved; p. 26 *(Nester and Dolphin)*, Niels Coogan, © 1991, reprinted with permission; p. 28, Neal A. Carlson; pp. 40, 50, 110, 114, Racquel Keller; p. 108, VIP © copyright, Redwing Shoes, reprinted with permission;. All other art is courtesy of the author.

Printed in the United States of America
00 99 98 97 96   10 9 8 7 6 5 4 3 2 1

*This workbook is dedicated to
my sister, Gail, who has slain many personal dragons
with a pen and paper.*

CONTENTS

FOREWORD

Of the great multitude of approaches developed for the purpose of gleaning insight, healing emotional wounds, and promoting psychospiritual growth, few are as practical and effective as journal writing. Those who have kept a diary or dream journal know the benefits of documenting and reflecting upon life's events, whether they be painful or joyful. Writing about them somehow puts them in proper perspective so that life's lessons can be learned and one's life truly becomes a spiritual journey.

Managing Stress, A Creative Journal provides the participant with over 75 nicely introduced journal themes that can be selected to reflect the person's immediate need, concern, emotional state, or sense of belonging. It serves as a valuable tool—always appropriate and always accessible. It is a book that can serve as life's little companion. Brian Luke Seaward's breadth of knowledge and deep sensitivity to the issues that we all face by simply being human comes through clearly.

If we truly are spiritual beings having a human experience, then Luke's book provides us with a simple roadmap to help guide us along the way.

MIROSLOV BORYSENKO
February 26, 1996

INTRODUCTION
THE IMPORTANCE OF JOURNAL WRITING

All sorrows can be borne, if you put them in a story.
Isak Dinesen

At the turn of the twentieth century, British East Africa, now known as Kenya, was a land ripe with adventure, from Mount Kilimanjaro to the Serengeti Plain. It attracted many an expatriate from the shores of Europe, Asia, and the Americas. Among these new citizens was the Dane Karen Blixen, the new wife of Baron Von Blixen, who settled down to carve a future life at the foot of the Ngong Hills, just outside Nairobi. A life of high adventure is not without its stressful episodes. In the seventeen years she spent in Africa, Karen contracted syphilis from an unfaithful husband, severed her relationship with him, and lost her farm to fire and her land to bankruptcy. Perhaps worst of all, she lost the one man she loved, Denys Finch Hatton, in the crash of a Gypsy Moth two-seater plane.

Throughout her life in Africa, Karen wrote. Writing and storytelling became a release, almost an escape; but in every case they were a means to cope with the changes that she encountered. Upon what she called an ungraceful return to her home in Denmark, Karen began to compose and organize the memories of her African adventures. The result was a wonderful collection of personal experiences intertwining the sad with the sublime, written under the pen name Isak Dinesen, to become the classic novel *Out of Africa*. While not everyone is a novelist, we all have life adventures that merit— often necessitate—a vehicle of expression that helps to ease the pain of the soul. In the words of Karen Blixen, "All sorrows can be borne, if you put them in a story."

To open up, share, and disclose feelings, perceptions, opinions, and memories has always been found to be therapeutic. Confessions of the mind can lighten the burden of the soul. Many religions have adapted this concept for spiritual healing. This is also the cornerstone upon which modern psychotherapy is based. Although conversation is the most common method of disclosure, writing down thoughts that occupy the mind is extremely therapeutic as well. Journal writing can be defined as a series of written passages that document the personal events, thoughts, feelings, memories, and perceptions in the journey throughout one's life leading to wholeness. Journal writing has proven to be a formidable coping technique to deal with stress, so much so that for years, psychologists and health educators alike have used journal writing as an awareness tool for self-exploration and enhancing personal development.

Often, there comes a time when our minds get overloaded with sensory stimulation and it seems that we cannot think straight. This is part of the "stress response"—unclear thinking due to sensory overload. The repercussions, including unfocused judgments, poor perspective, bad decision making, and eventual poor health, are dangerous. The cycle can become so strong that it never breaks. Actually, stress goes deeper than this. We live in an age where we hardly know ourselves at a profound level. We just don't take the time to examine our thoughts, feelings, perceptions, and attitudes. Not being honest with our true feelings leaves us empty-handed when we face life's daily stressors. In a world where change is perhaps the only constant factor, we need to stay continually in close touch with our thoughts, feelings, and perceptions to guide us through or around life's obstacles.

How does a journal fit in? The word *journal* comes from the root word *journee*, meaning a day's travel, or to journey or travel. Journals started as a means of guidance on long trips, an orientation record for a safe return passage. From Columbus to Lewis and Clark, to today's astronauts, journal writing has been and continues to be a proven means of personal guidance for each individual's journey through life. When pen or pencil is taken in hand and put to paper, a connection is made between the mind and the soul. Thoughts that are written down on paper make the author accountable for those thoughts. These thoughts become real, tangible, and focused; they become concrete. By taking the time to write down the thoughts and feelings that congest or trouble your mind, you develop a habit of clearing your mind of concerns, problems, and issues that constantly demand your attention. Unloading your thoughts can help clear the conscious mind. It also helps to initiate the resolution process in dealing with life's stressors. When personal issues are written down, not only is there a cathartic effect, but often insight into the resolution of these problems begins to unfold.

How does journal writing relate to stress management? Quite simply, the best stress management program deals with both the causes and symptoms of stress. Relaxation techniques are great for dealing effectively with the signs and symptoms of stress (e.g., ulcers, migraines, and hypertension). If, however, you give attention only to the symptoms of stress and not the causes of the perceived tension, then relaxation techniques are only a temporary solution to a chronic problem. The best way to deal with the cause of your stress is to first increase your awareness of what your stressors are. What is really bothering you? You cannot put strategies into action if the real cause of your problems is fogged in within the depths of your mind.

Journal writing opens the doors to your conscious mind and allows you to really examine what you are feeling—where you have traveled in the course of a day, and where this journey has taken you with your own mental, emotional, and spiritual growth and development. By writing in your journal for a period of weeks or months, and then reading through these passages of your life's journey, you will begin to see specific patterns to your thinking, your emotional responses, and even your actions and behaviors; patterns that are unnoticeable on a day-to-day basis. This is where the real self-learning process takes place. From this ability to see patterns in your thoughts and behaviors you can get a better bearing on how to deal with the issues and concerns that cause stress. Current research suggests that not only is journal writing good for the soul, but it is also good for the body. Studies by James Pennebaker in which individuals kept journals and wrote about their frustrations and painful experiences revealed that, over time, they had fewer physical ailments (e.g., headaches, cramps, and colds), suggesting a new bond in the link between mind and body.

The idea for this journal workbook came from a series of homework assignments that I gave to my students as exercises in self-awareness to deal with perceived stress. Actually, the origins for these assignments came from a workshop I attended several years ago on self-reflection. One of the workshop experiences, based on a book by Anne Morrow Lindbergh entitled *Gift from the Sea*, involved selecting a seashell from a basket loaded with all kinds of objects from the ocean floor. The shell then served as a tool for introspection; by centering, focusing on, and touching the shell we could focus and get in touch with ourselves. Although there was no writing involved, I liked the idea so much that I adapted it for my own stress management class as an in-class journal assignment. It became an instant hit. Other journal themes followed.

Since then I have searched for other similar experiences and have included these in the workbook as well. With particular interest I share the theme of the Vision Quest. On a recent trip back home to Colorado, I discovered the native American tradition of the Vision Quest. I found it to be a very moving experience, and this too I adapted for the workbook. As an in-class journal assignment, it also has become quite popular because it also reaches to the depths of one's soul. Other assignments were inspired from a great many books I have read (see References section listed at the back of the workbook for further reading on self-discovery). Generally, I have found that, depending on where each person is in his or her life journey, certain journal themes hold greater significance. I have tried to create an assortment of topics, issues, and concerns that I have experienced in my own life as well as those I have encountered through the lives of my students, clients, and workshop participants.

At first, journal writing can seem tedious and difficult. This often occurs when you are not in the habit of articulating your innermost feelings. But after a while, as with any skill, you become better at it. Included are many suggested journal theme entries to help you get started with this process to enhance your journal writing and self-awareness skills. These theme entries serve to motivate and maintain the writing process. They were created to serve as catalysts for soul searching as well as to give you a jump start when you need writing motivation. However, you are strongly encouraged to write on your own with no other theme than "What's on my mind today"? There is no particular order to the selected journal themes. Although these subjects are outlined in the table of contents, you may begin with any journal theme, or simply write on anything that you feel is important and merits your attention. It is important to remember that when you write, write of yourself and for yourself, not to others or for others. The contents of this journal aren't for publication. They are confidential (unless perhaps, they are assigned for a class or workshop). Your thoughts should be articulated yet unedited. When you begin to accept this premise your writing becomes much easier and more honest, and the rewards are more fruitful.

When is the best time to write? This varies from person to person. The end of the day is often an ideal time, but perhaps this is not convenient, given your schedule. You really have to decide for yourself. Journal writing time, however, should be uninterrupted time, quality alone time. How often should you take pen in hand and write? It is suggested that the benefits of journal writing are realized when there is continuity with journal entries. A good goal to start with is a minimum of three entries per week. Moreover, journal entries don't always have to be filled with thoughts and descriptions of stressful events based on fear or anger. They can recount good times as well. Life is a combination of positive and negative experiences and your journal should reflect this. Mostly, by keeping a regular habit of journal writing you really begin to know yourself well, and eventually, in the process, become your own best friend.

Best wishes and inner peace,
BRIAN LUKE SEAWARD
Boulder, Colorado

JOURNAL SUMMARY
EXCERPTS

The following are some excerpts from journal summaries that I have come across in my several years of teaching college students and journal writing workshops. These might serve as an inspiration to keep a journal on a regular basis.

"The journal helped me to identify what my values are. I found that my values are somewhat different than I had originally thought. I always made the assumption that my beliefs were the same as those of my parents. Although there is some validity to this, there are some areas where my values differ from theirs. Through the use of my journal, I learned how important value definition is in how I perceive things. The last trend that I noticed in my journal was the increasing number and effectiveness of my options for reducing stress. At the beginning, I didn't have any; but as time went on, I came up with better options. I took this to mean that I was learning something—I hope so."

"For a long time now, I've known what stresses me the most. It has been a long time since I've been able to confide in or let anyone get really close to me. I've been so wrapped up in school for the past eight years of my life, and it's really getting lonely. As time goes on, it gets harder and harder to express myself. In a sense, I'm scared of situations because I don't know how I'll react. In this aspect I don't know myself very well and I'm afraid to find out. This journal has really helped me get in touch with myself."

"This stress reduction journal offered no cure-all for my problems, but it gave me valuable help. It helped me understand and see what I thought. By knowing what was going through my mind, I began to realize things about myself, some things I might have never known. A common phrase I saw within my journal was 'good enough.' The paper was 'good enough,' the letter I wrote home was 'good enough,' I was doing things so they would be 'good enough' and in doing so, not achieving my potential. I was striving for mediocrity. I'm trying to break this bad habit and I think I have made a little headway. Creativity is now more clear and interesting to me than ever before. I found myself writing short stories in my journal or just creating ideas for work or pleasure."

"When I divorced my husband of seven years, I cried on everyone's shoulder for months. That was a year ago. But people get tired of the same old complaints, even your best friends. So I took refuge in writing in my journal. It served as a great sounding board. It certainly helped me heal some very deep wounds. I've learned that there are some thoughts that are best left between my mind and the pages of a journal notebook."

"Toxic thoughts! I didn't know I harbored so many of these. I really thought I held an optimistic attitude, but I saw that there is a strong correlation between certain negative attitudes and their corresponding stressors. When the thoughts find their way onto paper, they tend to lose their toxic effects in my body. Over the past three months I've seen some things in myself that I often dislike in others. Humm! Very therapeutic. By the way, there were a lot of good times I was reminded of and I'm glad that I have some details to fall back on on occasion. I even found myself laughing out loud."

"Things have always bugged me, but I was never sure what. The journal helped me realize that several things really bugged me and led me to a way to solve my problems. This may sound trivial,

but it used to cause me no end of pain. When someone is bothering me and that person asked me 'What's wrong?' I always answer, 'Nothing.' I automatically think they should know what is wrong, but I am wrong in thinking this. I have learned that it bugs me to not tell people they are bothering me. This may seem like a trivial point but I found it a very interesting realization."

"Keeping a journal has revealed that I am insecure and unsure about a great many things [and] I have been putting a false facade on to cover up these feelings. I sometimes think too much, and I often don't think at all. This emotional predicament may cause other people trouble, but I am beginning to take some comfort in my humanness. I look at it this way; someone once said, 'Poetry is mass confusion understood.' At times my mind is mass confusion. Through my journal if I can begin to understand it, I'll be poetry in motion."

ACKNOWLEDGMENTS

This workbook has seen many incarnations, most notably in its five years under the title of *My Best Friend: A Creative Journal for Stress Management*. I am most grateful to Jones and Bartlett Publishers for their interest in publishing this in conjunction with *Managing Stress: Principles and Strategies for Health and Wellbeing*. There are several people I would like to thank for nurturing this project throughout the years. To Joe Burns, Paula Carroll, Mary Cervantes Sanger, Judy Songdahl, Anne Benaquist, Rafael Millán, and Suzanne Crane at Jones and Bartlett, thanks for your assistance in the publication of this workbook. To Paige Erikson and Michael Dalrymple, thank you so much for your tutorials on the Macintosh; I owe you both another dinner. To Lonnie Dalrymple, thanks for being another set of eyes—all sorrows *can* be borne, right? To Diana Dee Tyler, who over the years I have most affectionately called "The Bear Lady," thank you for giving me permission to use your wonderful pieces of art *Three Bears Heads*, *Sea Otter*, and *Monarch Butterfly*. To Niels Coogan, thanks for permission to reprint *Nestor* and *Dolphin*. To my sister, Gail, and my dear friends Roger Navis, Racquel Keller, and Sam Campagna, thank you so much for your artwork which enhances these pages, bringing the journal themes to life. Thanks to Susan Griffin, my assistant, who went over each word with a fine tooth comb. Special thanks to Miron Borysenko for your kind words in the Foreword. I am indebted to my mentors and colleagues, who have served as a great inspiration on my own path of enlightenment: Elisabeth Kübler-Ross, Roger von Oech, Patricia Norris, Larry Dossey, Joan Borysenko, Bernie Siegel, Carl Jung, and Jean Shinoda Bolen, to name just a few. And finally, thanks to my support network—Bonnie Montgomery, Mary Jane Mees, Skylar Sherman, Rob Sleamaker, Donna and Scott Mefford, Neal and Rita Carlson, Linda Campanelli, Jo Safrit, Susan Moran, Ingrid Helvig, Andy Frank, Betsy Meholick, Mark Ricard, Doug Backland, Dan and Michelle Parent, Laurie Caswell, Dan Ault, Donna Nelson, Pat and Caleb O'Connor, Sandy Ungar, Kathleen Zevala, Jane Searles, Katy Thurston, Karen Abbot, Nan Adams, Tom Sarson, Craig Broaderdorp, and Steve Fitzgerald—for your inspiration and friendship; and all my students at the American University, the University of Northern Colorado, and the University of Colorado, who have been wonderful teachers in their own right.

JOURNAL THEMES

1

TOP TEN STRESSORS

There are many surveys, assessments, and questionnaires to help people identify circumstances that cause stress and the intensity of frustration that they create. But these questionnaires can be quite impersonal and, typically, they tell us what we already know–that indeed we do have stress. But oftentimes people are not aware of what the cause of their stress is because they don't take the time to examine it. More often than not, people ignore or avoid their stressors, hoping they will go away. Seldom, if ever, does this approach work, and usually these problems don't go away. In fact, they usually haunt us until we take some positive action.

The best way to start to get a handle on the cause of your stress is to pinpoint exactly what is bothering you. By writing down what is on your mind you begin to get a better idea of what it's all about. So take a moment to think about what is on your mind, what is troubling you, or what caused you to get angry or afraid of something lately. Make a list and then prioritize your top ten stressors from the most stressful to the least stressful. If you have fewer than ten, fine. Don't feel compelled to add more than you really have. Once you have made this list, describe each stressor in a couple of sentences so you have a really good focus on each one.

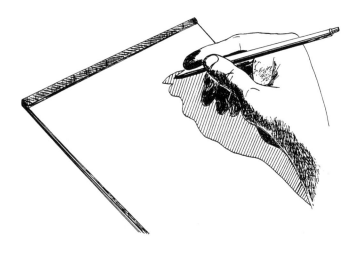

2

WHO AM I?

Who am I? This is, perhaps, the hardest question we will ever encounter in the course of our lives. We wear many hats, play many roles, and wear many faces, sometimes all in the course of one day. If our environments were constant throughout life, the answer might seem easier, but we live in a dynamic world where change is constant. Some would advocate that we are our current identities, while others might say that we are a collection of all our experiences. Perhaps the truth lies somewhere in between.

Take a moment to think about who and all that you really are. What roles do you play (student, roommate, son, daughter, mother, father, colleague, confidant, supervisor, neighbor, spouse, brother, sister, friend) and what is (are) the major role(s)? What makes up your current identity, what do you identify or associate yourself with, and what are the most significant experiences (good, bad, or ugly) that have contributed to your own makeup? Then articulate your thoughts on paper. Because change is constant, your answer today will most likely be different than your answer yesterday or tomorrow. But by beginning to understand who and all that we are, we can see ourselves from a broader perspective, seeing the whole rather than fragmented pieces that distort this self-perspective. With a clear focus on who we are, we often gain a better handle on the challenges and concerns that enter our lives in this constantly changing world.

Who are you?

3

OPTIMIST OR PESSIMIST?

You should always be aware that your head creates your world.
Ken Keyes

Some people are optimists and some are pessimists. Many people fall somewhere in between. In your opinion, describe the difference between an optimist and a pessimist, and give an example of each. Then explain which side you see yourself on most of the time and why.

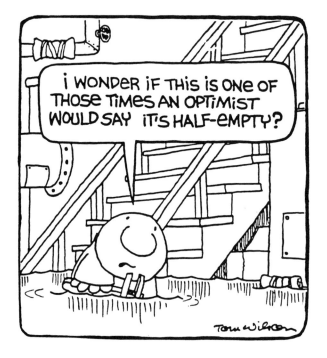

4

SELF-TALK

Take a moment to eavesdrop on your thoughts. If you are like most people, the thoughts that go through your head are skewed toward the negative side of life. Listen! The channels of thought that span the spectrum of frequencies in the mind can be compared to frequencies on a radio. As such, the negative self-talk is analogous to the dominant station your mind is stuck on. Using this metaphor, you can see that if your mind has a tendency to play the pre-recorded message of negativity, you have the ability to reprogram the station and train your mind to listen to another voice, just as you would change the station of a car radio.

1. What does your negative voice tell you about yourself?

2. Do the thoughts of your negative voice become words that pass through your lips to downgrade yourself or others? If so, why do you suppose you do this?

3. It is quite common to change radio stations in the car while driving. What steps can you take to change your thoughts?

5

HOW WAS YOUR DAY TODAY?

The measure of mental health is the disposition to find good everywhere.
Ralph Waldo Emerson

"How was your day today?" This is a standard question that wives, husbands, parents, children, or any loved ones pose to the working force as they return home from the office, dock, school, factory, or road. Now it is time to ask it of yourself. To sum up your day is a way to unload your mind from sensory overload, as well as to help you identify and come to terms with the major issues and concerns experienced in the course of your day.

So, how was your day? Good or bad? Did any significant events (positive or negative) occur? How do you feel about them?

6

VISION QUEST

Our lives are a series of events strung together through the spirit of each breath and heartbeat. Some events are more significant than others, as they mark powerful changes in the growth and development of our existence. In earlier cultures as far back as the dawn of humankind, these events of change, these transitions from one life stage to another, were referred to as *rites of passage*. These rites often included a ceremony of celebration. Today, these are often continued in practices including bar mitzvahs, weddings, baby showers, and funerals.

In modern American culture, the importance of personal rites of passage has been de-emphasized or forgotten. Attention is placed on the ceremony without true recognition of its purpose. In reality, many of our major life events are done alone with no supportive guidance, no community involvement, and no celebration. Modern technology has also replaced our sense of origin, leaving us uncentered and ungrounded. The result often leaves us unable to deal effectively with the stress produced from life's crises or without the maturity to advance through the developmental stages of life.

In the tradition of the native American Indian, a Vision Quest marks a significant rite of passage. It is a wilderness retreat where one reflects on one's inner resources as well as reaffirms one's centeredness and connection to Mother Earth. In a Vision Quest, the individual seeks a vision of a meaningful purpose in life and gains a greater understanding of himself or herself from within. This concept has been adopted as a cornerstone to the nation's Outward Bound program: self-reliance through introspection in nature. A Vision Quest marks a major life transition. Those who initiate this quest search for a vision to guide them through the transition period of change. Although in the truest sense, a Vision Quest is done in the solitude of the wilderness, you can initiate this process anywhere. The following questions are provided to lead you on the first steps of your Vision Quest.

1. What significant events to date would you consider to be rites of passage in your life? Why do you consider these to be rites of passage for you?

2. Take a moment to ask yourself what life event you are in the midst of. What dragons are you battling with right now? What life passage are you entering or emerging from? Rites of passage are thought to have three distinct phases. As you ponder these questions, follow these phases of the Vision Quest:

a. **Severance:** A separation from old ways—of familiar lifestyle, habits, perhaps even people.

b. **Threshold:** The actual quest, a search for a vision or understanding of this transition, an inventory of inner resources and external surroundings to provide guidance through the transition period.

c. **Incorporation:** A return from the quest to the community, with new insight and the ability to apply the knowledge from this experience as you progress in the development of your life.

3. During a Vision Quest, one receives the gift of a name to symbolize connectedness and groundedness. What name does the wind whisper in your ears?

7

GUIDED MENTAL IMAGERY

One relaxation technique for stress management is called guided mental imagery. In this technique, you think of a peaceful, calm image that promotes relaxation throughout your mind and body. To make it effective, you employ the imagination of not only your visual sense but that of sound, smell, and touch as well. The combined creative effort of these sensations actually places you at the scene and promotes a deeper sense of relaxation. When people think of peaceful scenes, they usually think of a natural setting, somewhere where everyday problems are put in perspective with nature. It is no wonder that people take vacations in magnificent natural settings like fabulous island beaches, majestic mountain peaks, or lone ocean dunes. The best scenes seem to be far away from the crowds and concerns of our everyday world, providing a retreat to nurture the soul.

Now it's time for you to use your creative thoughts and create some mental images of scenes that you feel are examples of perfect peaceful retreats. Describe five mental images or peaceful, relaxing scenes that you would like to escape to momentarily. Use all your senses to place yourself at each scene. Be as elaborate with the description as you can so that each image can remain vivid in your memory.

8

DREAMS
THE LANGUAGE OF SYMBOLS

Dreams are a powerful language. They offer insight into the shadows of our unconscious mind. Carl Jung, world-renowned psychologist and a pioneer in dream analysis, stated that dreams offer a basis of psychic balance if only we would take the time to become more aware of them and reflect on their meaning. Although often expressed in a language of symbols, dreams may offer insight into ways to resolve our current problems. This insight begins with an awareness of dream fragments, followed by an interpretation process. As Jung suggested, the dream cannot be separated from the dreamer, and indeed, each of us is best suited to interpret our own dreams. A full interpretation, however, comes from looking at the dream image from every perspective to try to understand its meaning.

To enhance this awareness of dreams, try leaving your journal by your nightstand and remind yourself before you fall asleep that you want to remember your dreams. Upon first waking, record whatever dream images or fragments you can recall. Then mull over these images and listen to the thoughts they suggest. You may wish to revisit these dream images because their meaning is not always obvious. Experts agree that not all dreams are significant, but the act of recording your images from the dream state may help you to deal more effectively with concerns and issues that you confront in your waking hours.

What recent dream do you recall that seemed significant? Do any objects that you recall seem to offer personal symbolism? After thinking about the fragments or sequences, do they begin to make any sense to you?

9

CREATIVE PROBLEM SOLVING

Imagination is more powerful than knowledge.
Albert Einstein

The world has seven continents. Seven land masses. Seven environments. Although we each live on the same planet, we often have a special focus of our own world. As our world turns, we have different environments that ground our experiences, often many in the same day: the home environment, the work environment, the family environment, the play environment, and our natural environment, to name a few.

1. What do the continents of your world look like? How many continents or environments do you have? How large and where are they in relationship to each other with regard to importance in your life? Try making a sketch of the continents of your world, giving yourself a global view of your collective environments.

2. Just as international events capture our attention, sometimes causing us concern, frustration, or worry, so do our personal events or stressors that arise on the continents of our own world. Some continents, like Australia, may be very dormant or peaceful, while others, like Europe, are quite active. Take a moment to scan the continents of your life and make a list of the major headline stressors in each of your environments.

3. Many times when we are faced with a problem that stresses us, we tend to think of only one way to handle it. The ways we select are not always effective (e.g., avoidance, repression, hostility, or immobilization). But often, if not always, there are several ways to effectively deal with our problems. We just have to be creative. Creativity involves two phases: a *germination* phase, where imagination is employed to create an idea, and a *harvest* phase, where a creative strategy is formulated to make the idea become a reality. In the germination phase, one explores for new ideas and then manipulates these ideas to one's environment. In the harvest phase, one judges the practicality of these ideas as viable options and then champions the cause with the most viable solution. Using your sense of creative thinking (both a germination and a harvest phase), think of two new viable options to successfully deal with one stressor in each environment.

10

A GIFT FROM THE SEA

Individuals are so very different, yet we all share so many common features, thoughts, even perceptions. Our makeup is so complex, yet similar, from one person to another. We all have qualities that we consider either strengths or weaknesses, and these certainly vary from person to person. Strengths can be magnified to bolster self-esteem. Weaknesses, too, can be magnified and become roadblocks to our human potential. The world is full of metaphors regarding the facets of our lives. For example, a seashell can be considered a metaphor, a symbol of ourselves.

After an extremely stressful event that changed the life of Anne Morrow Lindbergh and her husband, Charles, Anne took refuge on a secluded beach to find peace of mind and solace in her heart. In her book *Gift from the Sea*, Lindbergh shares her personal thoughts as she cradled a series of seashells in the palms of her hands and reflected on the images they suggested, as well as on the symbolism each offered.

The following thoughts and questions inspired by Lindbergh's book are provided to help you explore this shell metaphor. You don't need to have a seashell in hand to do this exercise, but sometimes something tangible can really open up your thoughts.

1. Pick a shell from a collection of shells (real or imaginary) and hold it in your hand for a moment. Close your eyes and really feel it. What was it that attracted you to this particular shell? Take a moment to describe the shell you picked: its color, shape, texture, and size.

2. Many sea creatures have shells. Some have beautifully colored shells while some have incredible detail with ridges, points, and curls. Some shells are quite small, and others are very big. Some shells are very fragile while others seem the epitome of strength. Like sea creatures, we too have shells, though they are not quite as obvious. What is your shell like? Describe its shape, color, texture, and any other features that you wish to include—features that differentiate it from other shells.

3. A shell serves a purpose for a sea creature. It acts as a home as well as a form of protection; a base for security. The shells we have also act as a means of protection. Our shells, too, can offer a form of strength and security, but they can also overprotect. Does your own shell overprotect, or is it a growing shell?

4. We all have strengths and weaknesses. Strengths are strong points of our personality or attributes that bring us favorable attention. Weaknesses, on the other hand, are what we perceive as our faults, insecurities, or attributes that we associate with negative connotations. List your strengths and beside this list write your weaknesses. Now take a careful look at this list. Sometimes strengths can actually be weaknesses while some weaknesses can be disguised as our strong points. For example, take a person who is well organized. This could be considered a weakness if it spills over into perfectionism. Sometimes what we see as our weaknesses others see as our strengths, and this may in fact be true. Many times it is the perceptions that make this difference. Now take a look at your list again. Are any of your strengths potential weaknesses and/or vice versa?

5. Feel free to add any comments, feelings, and even memories to this journal entry.

20

11

SYNCHRONICITY

A coincidence is God's way of remaining anonymous.
Bernie Seigel

Have you ever been in one of those situations where you thought to yourself, "This is not just a coincidence; there is something significant if not mystical going on here"? Perhaps it was getting a phone call from a troubled friend the instant you picked up the phone to call that very person. Or perhaps it was a time when you changed seats on a plane so a husband could sit next to his wife and you ended up sitting next to someone who weeks later offered you a job.

A coincidence is often described as the coming together of two random events. Sometimes we just shrug off the confluence of like events as meaningless, but often there is a message underlying these events, begging us to take notice. As Bernie Siegel says, "A coincidence is God's way of remaining anonymous."

Actually, a coincidence of significance goes by another name. Psychologist Carl Jung coined the word *synchronicity* to explain significant events that coincide with meaning. The importance of this new word, he explained, was to underscore that two or more circumstances of this nature are not random events, colliding in time by chance. Rather, their relevance is a message, and we should pay attention to it. Unlike the mechanistic view of life, which tends to deny a higher order to the universe, Jung believed that there is a divine order to our lives even if we are not at a point where we can observe it. To paraphrase Jung's words, synchronicity is a message from the divine consciousness. If we can begin to move beyond the amazement of coincidences, the next step is to search for meaning, however significant or trivial, in the two events which come together before us.

If we make ourselves more aware, we will notice many moments of synchronicity. Have you noticed any lately? What were the circumstances in which you encountered these events? After pondering this matter for a moment, can you detect any significance in the synchronicity before you? If not lately, can you recall any episodes of synchronicity of major relevance to you earlier in your life? What do you suppose they mean? Describe them here.

12

VALUES ASSESSMENT AND CLARIFICATION

Values—those abstract ideals that shape our lives. Values are constructs of importance. They give the conscious mind structure. They can also give countries and governments structure. The U.S. Declaration of Independence is all about values, including "life, liberty, and the pursuit of happiness." Although values are intangible, they are often symbolized by material objects or possessions, which can make values very real. Some everyday examples of values are love, peace, privacy, education, freedom, happiness, creativity, fame, integrity, faith, friendship, morals, health, justice, loyalty, honesty, and independence.

Where do values come from? We adopt values at a very early age, unconsciously, from people whom we admire, love, or desire acceptance from, like our parents, brothers and sisters, school teachers, and clergy. Values are often categorized into two groups: *basic* values, a collection of three to five instrumental values that are the cornerstones of the foundation of our personalities, and *supporting* values, which augment our basic values. Throughout our development we construct a value system, a collection of values that influences our attitudes and behaviors, all of which make up our personality.

As we mature, our value systems also change because we become accountable for the way we think and behave. Like the earth's tectonic plates, our values shift in importance, causing our own earth to quake. These shifts are called *value conflicts* and they can cause a lot of stress. Classic examples of value conflicts include love vs. religious faith or social class (Romeo and Juliet), freedom vs. responsibility, and work vs. leisure (the American Dream). Conflicts in values can be helpful in our own maturing process if we work through the conflict to a full resolution. Problems arise when we ignore the conflict and avoid clarifying our value system. The purpose of this journal theme is for you to take an honest look at your value system, assess its current status, and clarify unresolved issues associated with values in conflict. The following are some questions to help you in the process of values assessment and clarification.

1. Make a list of the core values you hold (values come from things that give you meaning and importance, yet they are abstract in nature).

2. See if you can identify which of these values are *basic*, or instrumental, at this point in your life and which *support* or augment your basic values.

3. How are your values represented in your possessions (e.g., a BMW may represent wealth or freedom)?

4. Describe how your values influence your dominant thoughts, attitudes and beliefs.

5. Do you have any values that compete for priority with one another? If so, what are they, and why is there a conflict?

6. What do you see as the best way to begin to resolve this conflict in values? Ask yourself if it is time to change the priority of your values or perhaps discard values that no longer give importance to your life.

13

ONE
A HOLY MOMENT

Have you ever experienced a moment in your life where you became one with the universe? A special moment, a natural high, or a singular sensation that took your breath away and filled your heart with so much joy and wonder that you wanted to reach out, grab the world, and hug it? Most likely you have had a few singular sensations; more if you're lucky.

Psychologist Abraham Maslow called these *peak experiences*. Stress researcher Joan Borysenko refers to them as *holy moments,* and indeed they are very special. Like Maslow, Borysenko is of the opinion that not only do we need to be more receptive to these experiences, but that we also need to occasionally remind ourselves of these events to help lend emotional balance to the negative experiences we encounter throughout our lives. Search your memory bank. What holy moment comes to your mind at the thought of this suggestion? Perhaps it was seeing a deer jump into a thicket of woods while you were jogging on a dirt road, or standing on a mountain top watching the sun reflect its crimson colors on a blanket of clouds near the horizon. Maybe it happened while making contact with a long-lost friend or hugging your favorite dog or cat after a really bad day.

Close your eyes for a moment and think back to a very special moment when you felt a profound if not divine connection to the universe—a moment that transcended your everyday feelings and responsibilities. Try to recall the emotional sensation that you experienced with this event. Then open your eyes and try to recapture the event on paper in as much detail as possible.

14

ANGER
THE FIGHT EMOTION

He who angers you, conquers you.
Elizabeth Kenny

Anger. The word itself brings to mind images of pounding fists, yelling, and smoke pouring out of one's ears and nose. But anger is as natural a human emotion as love. It is universal among all humans. Anger is a survival emotion; it's the fight component of the fight-or-flight response. We use anger to communicate our feelings, from impatience to rage. We employ anger to communicate boundaries and defend values. Studies show that the average person has fourteen to fifteen anger episodes a day. These often arise when our expectations are not met upon demand. Although feeling angry is within the normal limits of human emotions, it is often mismanaged and misdirected. Unfortunately, we have been socialized to suppress our feelings of anger. As a result, anger either tears us apart from the inside (ulcers) or promotes intermittent eruptions of verbal or physical violence. In most, if not all, cases we do not deal with our anger correctly.

Research has shown that there are four very distinct ways in which people mismanage their anger:

1. **Somatizers:** People who never show any signs of anger and internalize their feelings until eventually there is major bodily damage (e.g., ulcers, temporomandibular joint syndrome [TMJ], colitis, or migraines).

2. **Self-punishers:** People who neither repress their anger nor explode, but rather deny themselves a proper outlet of anger due to guilty feelings (e.g., eating, shopping).

3. **Exploders:** Individuals who erupt like a volcano and spread their temper like hot lava, destroying anyone and anything in their path with either verbal or physical abuse.

4. **Underhanders:** Individuals who sabotage or seek revenge to get even with someone through somewhat socially acceptable behavior (e.g., sarcasm, appearing late for meetings).

Although we tend to employ all of these styles at one time or another, given the situation and prevailing circumstances, we tend to rely on one dominant style of mismanaged anger. What is your most dominant style? What situations provoke an anger response in you? How do you deal with these feelings of anger?

There are some ways to deal with anger correctly or perhaps even creatively. For example: (1) take a time-out from the situation, followed by a time-in to resolve the issue, (2) communicate your feelings diplomatically, (3) learn to think through your anger, (4) plan several options to a situation, (5) lower personal expectations, and most importantly, (6) learn to forgive—make past anger pass. What are some ways you can vent your anger creatively?

Although anger is an emotion we all experience and should recognize when it arises, it is crucial to manage anger correctly. Sometimes just writing down on paper what gets you frustrated can be the beginning of the resolution process. And anger must be resolved.

15

FEAR
THE FLIGHT EMOTION

"We have nothing to fear but fear itself." Those immortal words spoken by Franklin D. Roosevelt during the Great Depression were expressed to calm an unsettled American public. Fear, like anger, is a very normal human emotion. We all experience it in our lives and more often than not, too many times in the course of our lives. Unlike anger, fear tends to be a difficult emotion to resolve. Feelings of anxiety or fear can trickle down from the mind to the body and wreak physical havoc from head to toe. While anger tends to make one want to defend turf and fight, fear makes one want to head for the hills and keep on running. The effects of fear can be exhausting. In fact, the effects do exhaust the body to the point of disease, illness, and sometimes death. Avoidance isn't the answer, but it's often the most frequently employed technique used to deal with fear.

Although many situations can promote anxiety, there are really only a handful of basic human fears that these situations fall under. They include the following:

1. **Fear of failure:** A loss of self-worth through an event or action that promotes feelings of self-rejection.

2. **Fear of rejection:** A loss of self-worth due to a perceived lack of acceptance from someone you consider important.

3. **Fear of the unknown:** A fear based on a lack of inner faith to act without knowledge of future events or circumstances.

4. **Fear of dying:** A fear of the pain, suffering, and uncertainty of death that produces anxiety.

5. **Fear of isolation:** A fear of loneliness; discomfort at being alone.

6. **Fear of loss of self-control:** The inability to determine which factors are and are not controllable, and a sense of not being able to manage many circumstances in one's life.

Many of these basic human fears are very closely related and may overlap in some instances. Some fears may also dominate our way of thinking while others are unrelated to our lifestyles. Fear of any kind, however, is very much related to our level of self-esteem. When we are down on ourselves we are most susceptible to situations or circumstances that we perceive as fearful. Like anger, fears must be resolved. Resolution does not result from ignoring or avoiding the problem. It is not easy and it takes work. When pursued properly, resolution is a continual process with many fruitful outcomes.

Sometimes by looking at our stressors, we can determine which fears they are associated with. The following questions may help you reflect on your current stressors that fall into this category.

1. Does one of these basic human fears tend to dominate your list of stressors? If so, why do you suppose that is the case?

2. How do you usually deal with your fears? Are you the type of person who hopes the circumstances surrounding these fears will go away?

3. What are some ways that will help you deal with some of these major fears?

30

16

MY PERSONAL TOTEM POLE

In the Pacific Northwest, native Americans established a long-standing tradition of storytelling by carving out of long wooden poles facial features of people and animals that represented a particular spirit or character of importance. The order in which they appeared on the pole unfolded into a special sequence of events which illustrated the highlights of a very important story. Some totem poles described tribal legends, stories of creation, mythology, and mystical happenings, while others related specific historical events of a family's heritage. The totem pole was a way to preserve the personal history.

Each totem pole is unique because the story told is based on the particular people, animals, or spirits that brought influence or inspiration to a particular tribe, family, or individual. We each have our own historical story to tell that is also marked by certain events, objects, and people who have touched our lives. Personal totem poles might include special symbols that represent important events, serving as personal landmarks, perhaps even as guides, in the journey of our lives.

A maple leaf
A golden retriever
A sailboat
Cowboy boots
A passport
A wedding ring

If you were to carve (describe) your life story on a long pole of wood, highlighting those symbols that represent the significant points that you remember in your life journey, what would they be? Take a few moments to sketch out your own totem pole that tells your personal history, and then relate this story, linking these symbolic images on paper so that one day it may be passed down through the generations of your own family.

17
MANDALA OF THE HUMAN SPIRIT

A *mandala* is a circular-shaped object symbolizing unity with four separate quarters that represent directions of the universe, seasons of the years, or four points of reference. The origin of the mandala can be traced back to the dawn of humankind. Mandalas vary in size, design, colors, and symbolism. They are often used in meditation as a focal point of concentration. In addition they are used as decorations in many cultures from the Native American medicine wheel to art depictions from the Far East.

The mandala of the human spirit is a symbol of wholeness. It is a tool of self-awareness to allow you the opportunity to reflect on some of the components of the human spirit: a meaningful purpose in your life, personal values, and the implicit chance to learn more about yourself in precious moments of solitude. Each quadrant represents a direction of your life with a symbol of orientation. The east is the initial point of origin. It represents the rising sun, the point of origin for each day. The focus of the mandala then moves southward, then to the west, and finally to the north.

Each focal point of the mandala of the human spirit provides questions for reflection. Take a few moments to reflect on the directions of the mandala to get a better perspective on the wellbeing of your human spirit. Then draw a circle dividing it into four areas and fill in the answers to the respective questions, creating a mandala of your very own human spirit.

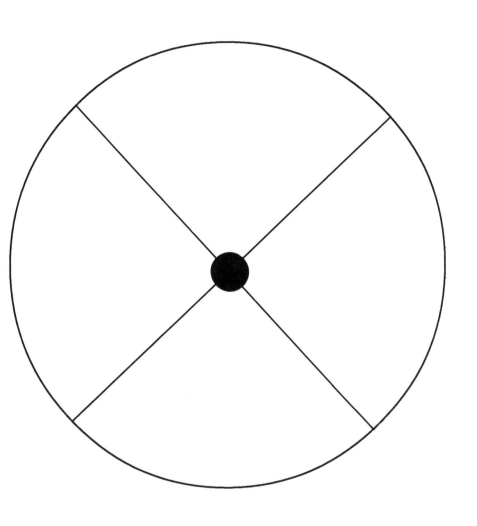

18

STICKS AND STONES

Is it true? Is it necessary? Is it kind?
Ancient Proverb

Remember the nursery school rhyme about sticks and stones? It goes like this: "Sticks and stones may break my bones, but names will never hurt me." Well, the truth is that names do hurt us—emotionally. When we are threatened by others, we tend to react rather than respond. Reacting with words is the most common way of venting anger, and the litany of negative words to choose from is endless. But negative words are as damaging as sticks and stones, perhaps even more so. Using mean words to avenge mean words is a contemporary way of taking an eye for an eye. The consequences are equally damaging for all parties involved.

There is an old Jewish parable that speaks to the nature of cruel words. In this story, a rabbi compares the tongue to an arrow. "Why an arrow?" asks one of his students. "Why not a sword?"

"Because," the rabbi explains, "If a man pulls out a sword to kill, whether it be friend or foe, pleas of mercy can make him change his mind to where he may return the sword to the sheath. But an arrow, once it's released from the bow, can never be returned, no matter how much one desires it."

Imagine for a moment that your thoughts and words are energy. Negative words (words that hurt), like arrows released from the bow, head straight for whomever you are talking about. Mean words wound. Good words heal. Although it may be impossible to retrieve an arrow, it is never too late to apologize. You cannot take words back, but in offering an apology the sting ends and the scar begins to heal. One of the most important inner resources in stress management is humility. When we react rather than respond out of stress, we only make our ego more vulnerable for more stress. Responding to stress requires a strong degree of humility.

1. What types of words, like arrows, shoot from your mouth toward other people? Are you very sarcastic or cynical?

2. Gossip is said to be the lowest form of communication. Are you a gossip? Do you sometimes speak ill of others?

3. How adept is your skill at apologizing? Are you able to say the words "I am sorry"?

4. Let's assume that your first inclination when stressed is to cut someone down, react with negative words, or gossip. What can you do to redirect your thoughts and neutralize your words so that these arrows stop in midflight or are deflected from their intended target because they are overtaken soon thereafter with words that heal.

Before you react with cruel words, start to gossip, or just try to cut someone down, remind yourself of these words from the ancient proverb: "Is it true? Is it necessary? Is it kind?"

19

INSPIRATION VS. INFLUENCE

Motivation is a complex phenomenon. It is thought to be comprised of two factors: those abstract qualities that inspire us from within, called *intrinsic* (e.g., faith, hope, love, and willpower), and those external factors, oftentimes more concrete in nature, that influence our way of thinking, our emotions, and subsequent behaviors, called *extrinsic* (e.g., money, rewards, trophies, people, and prizes). Although we are open to both types of motivation, some individuals tend to be more intrinsically motivated, while others are more influenced by external factors. Although both are natural characteristics of the human condition, generally people who find inspiration from within have a sustained quality of inner peace. Conversely, individuals who tend to be easily influenced are oftentimes less grounded and are consequently more susceptible to stress.

Part of the motivation puzzle is the concept of goals: creating a game plan, a strategy to promote and nurture our levels of inspiration. Additionally, creating personal rewards for achieving our goals can help reinforce motivational attitudes. Sometimes just knowing what factors motivate you can be helpful. These motivators can then be accessed when you are down in the dumps or in a rut, begging to be pulled out. Regarding personal influences, quite often we are not even aware of the factors and people who influence us. One reason why we are more susceptible to the influence of others than to our own free will is because inspiration takes work. Sometimes it seems easier to float with the tide than to swim.

Are you more intrinsically inspired or extrinsically motivated? What typically gets you out of bed and cruising down life's highway? What parts of life do you find to be inspiring? Are you the kind of person who makes goals and then rewards yourself for the accomplishments of these goals? What things, events, or happenings do you find really drain your energy level and/or self-esteem? What are some ways to boost your level of motivation and give yourself a jump start?

20

STRESS BAROMETER CHECK

Death is nature's way of saying slow down.
Woody Allen

Weather reports, economic forecasts, news sound bites, and mail are all bits of the information we assemble to gain a clearer understanding of our collective environments. Heart rate, blood pressure, ventilation, and muscle tension are clinical vital signs used to determine an initial health status report. Monitored regularly, they too can help us understand how our bodies absorb the events of our lives.

Sight, hearing, taste, smell, and touch are senses that help the mind gather and process the information that our environments send us. And too much information can overload the circuits. Figuratively speaking, this can blow a fuse. The result is stress-related disease and illness, from the common cold to coronary heart disease, and perhaps even cancer. Research now suggests that between 70 and 80 percent of all disease and illness is associated with stress. Therefore, it is a very good idea to monitor your stress levels periodically, as well as their potential repercussions on your body.

Take a moment to contemplate your mind-body relationship. Scope yourself top to bottom, head to toe, and check for any signs or symptoms that could be a result of too much wear and tear on the body from perceived stress. Are there any "hot spots"—some part of your body that is the target of your perceived stress? Next, check your current level of sensory input (deprivation vs. overload). Both can cause stress. If either seems to be evident, what can you do to remedy this situation? Take a pen in hand and jot down what you find with your stress barometer check.

Mental imagery can be a powerful tool to heal the body. From the research of O. Carl Simonton, coauthor of the best seller *Getting Well Again,* and Bernie Siegel, author of *Love, Medicine & Miracles*, we have learned that some cancer patients actually have had their tumors go into remission by thinking of metaphorical images to heal the body. Additional studies have shown that imagery can be used to assist in the healing processes of such health problems, including hypertension (imagining unclogged highways), ulcers (darning socks), tension headaches (ironing wrinkled clothes), you name it. All it takes is a little creativity—generating an idea and implementing the idea. If you have a hot spot or a manifestation of stress in your body, can you think of a metaphorical image to initiate the healing process? Give it a try. You may even want to map out this hot spot on an image of your body and write out a mental image to heal it.

40

21

DREAMS REVISITED

Although we all have dreams, remembering them is not always easy. But there are occasions when a certain dream is replayed in our mind over the course of months, perhaps even years. These recurring dreams may only have a short run on the mind's silver screen, or they may last throughout the course of our lifetime. These dreams, perhaps foggy in detail, surface occasionally in the conscious state, and the story they tell is all too familiar.

It is commonly believed that recurring dreams symbolize a hidden insecurity or a stressful event that has yet to be resolved. They don't have resolved endings. While there is much to the dream state that is still unknown, it is believed that dreams are images that the unconscious mind creates to communicate to the conscious mind in a language all its own. This form of communication is not a one-way street. Messages can be sent to the unconscious mind in a normal waking state as well.

Through the use of mental imagery, you can script the final scenes of a recurring dream with a happy ending. What seems to be the final scene of a dream is actually the beginning of the resolution process. The following is a true story: Once there was a young boy who had an afternoon paper route. One day while the boy was delivering papers, a large black German shepherd jumped out of the bushes and attacked him. The owner called the dog back, but not before the dog drew blood. As the boy grew into adulthood his love for dogs never diminished, but several times a year he awoke in a sweat from a recurring dream he had had once too often. **The Dream:** "It is dark and I am walking through the woods at night. Out from behind one of the trees comes this huge black dog. All I can see are his teeth, and all I can hear is his bark. I try to yell for help, but nothing comes out of my throat. Just as he lunges for me, I awake in a panic."

With a little thought and imagination, a final scene was drafted to bring closure to this dream story. **Final Scene:** "I am walking through the woods at night with a flashlight, a bone, and a can of mace. This time when the dog lunges at me, I shine the light in his eyes and spray mace in his face. He whines and whines, and then I tell him to sit. He obeys. I put the bone by his nose and he looks at me inquisitively. Then he licks the bone and starts to bite into it. I begin to walk away and the dog gets up to follow, bone in mouth. I stop and look back and he stops. He wags his tail. The sky grows light as the sun begins to rise, and the black night fades into pink and orange clouds. As I walk back to my house, I see the dog take his new find down the street. I open the door and walk upstairs and crawl back into bed." It has been five years, and this man has never had this dream again.

Ultimately we are the creators of our dreams. We are the writers, directors, producers, and actors of our dreams. Although drafting a final scene is no guarantee that the issues that produce recurring dreams are resolved, it is a great starting point in the resolution process, a time for reflection that may open up the channels of communication between the conscious and unconscious mind. Do you have a recurring dream that needs a final scene to be complete? Write out your recurring dream and give it a final scene.

22

ART THERAPY

Many of our thoughts and emotions are hard to express in words. Not always, but often a visual picture rich in color, texture, and style can best describe how we feel. Art therapy is used in many settings (hospitals, prisons, stress management classes, corporate executive wellness programs) to help individuals learn to express their thoughts and feelings visually, in a way that words cannot adequately describe. Many times drawings can communicate thoughts from the unconscious that the conscious mind can begin to decipher and understand for a more honest picture of the real you. For example, colors used and the proportion of objects or people can connote specific moods or personal meaning. Exploring thoughts, memories, and feelings from the right side of the brain can often lead to a clearer understanding of where these come from and perhaps what they represent. Illustrations, when combined with a narrative, can also be used to enhance memories of journal entries from vacations or special events.

What does it take to try this? Some desire and a little bit of imagination. You don't have to be an artist. You only need crayons, colored pencils, paint or pastels, some paper, and a desire to convey what's on your mind to paper. As children we love to draw, but as we get older we shy away from drawing because of fear of judgment. Like other journal assignments, this too is confidential. No one is going to look at it, no one is going to analyze or judge it, nor should you when you complete the picture. For this reason, there is no need to feel inhibited. Whether your skills produce stick figures or creations worthy of Rembrandt, give it a try.

The following suggestions are ideas used in art therapy classes. They are only suggestions. Feel free to adapt these in any way that you feel most comfortable.

1. With your eyes closed, draw a line on a page and then open your eyes and, from what you see, finish the picture to make whatever you would like.

2. Illustrate something that describes your best attributes or what best describes who you are, or draw yourself.

3. Identify one area of your body that you feel is a target organ, a recipient of your stress. From this, use your imagination to think up a mental image to cure or restore homeostasis to this part of your body and then draw this image on paper.

4. Draw a mandala. Your mandala. A mandala is like a personal coat of arms; in this case, a coat of arms of wholeness. Start with a circular shape and from this divide it into four equal (or unequal) areas. Add to this items or colors, or include anything that you feel gives you inspiration and wholeness (to be healthy means to be whole).

5. Draw a representation of your feelings of either anger or fear.

6. Draw whatever you like, whatever comes to mind, for whatever reason.

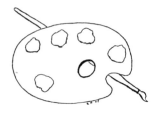

23

CONFRONTATION OF A STRESSOR

It happens to us all the time. Someone or something gets us frustrated, and we literally or figuratively head for the hills, either avoiding the person or thing altogether or ignoring the situation in the hope that it will go away. But when we ignore situations like this, they typically come back to haunt us. In the short run, avoidance looks appealing, even safe. But in the long run, it is bad policy. Really bad policy. We avoid confrontation because we want to avoid the emotional pain associated with it, the pain our ego suffers. Handled creatively, diplomatically, and rationally, the pain is minimal, and it often helps our spirits grow. After all, this is what life is all about: to achieve our full human potential.

The art of peaceful confrontation involves a strategy of creativity, diplomacy, and grace to ensure that you come out the victor, not the victim. In this sense, confrontation doesn't mean a physical battle but rather a mental, emotional, or spiritual battle. Unlike a physical battle where knights wear armor, this confrontation requires that you set aside the shield of your ego long enough to resolve the fear or anger associated with the stressor. The weapons of this confrontation are self-assertiveness, self-reliance, and faith. There is no malice, spite, or deceit involved. Coping mechanisms that aid the confrontation process include, but are not limited to, the following strategies: communication, information seeking, cognitive reappraisal, social engineering, and values assessment and clarification.

We all encounter stressors that we tend to run away from. Now it is time to gather your internal resources and make a plan to successfully confront your stressor. When you initiate this confrontation plan, you come out the victor with a positive resolution and a feeling of accomplishment. First, reexamine the list of your top ten stressors. Then, select a major stressor to confront and resolve. Prepare a plan of action, and then carry it out. When you return, write about it: what the stressor was, what your strategy was, how it worked, how you felt about the outcome, and perhaps most importantly, what you learned from this experience.

24

THINKING VS. FEELING

I think, therefore I am.
René Descartes

It has been said that we, as Americans, are out of touch with our feelings—literally. Out of touch, that is, until we reach a point where they beg to be listened to—a heart attack, a migraine headache, a backache, or a cancerous tumor.

If you were to ask the first ten people you come across how they felt about the government, the weather, the playoffs, the economy, or the arts, most likely each one would begin by saying *"Well, I think that..."* We are so conditioned to express ourselves intellectually rather than emotionally that we often stifle our emotional growth. This is not to say that thinking is bad. It's not! But more often than not, we are top-heavy in our thoughts and rather deficient in recognizing and expressing our feelings. As we all know by now, suppressing our feelings (especially unresolved negative emotions) can have a harmful effect on our health; in essence, a toxic effect on the body.

Are you a person who tends to express your thoughts more than your feelings? When asked how you feel about an issue, do you begin or continue your conversations with the phrase "I think that..."? The purpose of this journal theme (and entire journal) is to explore not just your thoughts but your feelings about your thoughts. "This makes me feel angry," "I feel exhilarated after finishing that project," or "I feel great being outdoors."

If you feel you need some practice with expressing your feelings, here are some topics in which you can begin to share your feelings here on paper.

1. How do you feel about the economy and the job market?
2. What are your feelings about the state of the global environment and the depletion of natural resources?
3. How do you feel about the current state of national politics?
4. What are your feelings about graduating next semester?
5. How do you feel about your current relationship (significant other)?
6. Try this exercise: On a blank piece of paper, draw a line down the middle and label the left side "Thoughts" and the right side "Feelings." Sit for ten minutes to think about an issue or problem and write down the thoughts and feelings you have as they surface in your mind, placing them on the corresponding sides of the paper.

25

MY POSITIVE ATTRIBUTES

Someone once calculated that the mineral contents and physiological properties of the human body have a net worth of approximately $2.65. Many estimates, however, have been calculated to appraise the real value of a human life with one unanimous decision: every human being is priceless. No monetary value can adequately replace us. No amount of money can compensate for the capabilities of the mind, body, and spirit. This fact alone would make you think that everyone has a lot going in his or her direction. In fact, we all do, it is just that more often than not it doesn't seem that way. We tend to dwell on our negative characteristics and this focus can really impede the quality of our lives. Perhaps the roots of American negativism can be traced to the dogma of Puritanism, which holds that personal worth is equal to the work you do, and no amount of work is ever enough. It's a fact, however, that Americans typically have a very negative attitude toward themselves. Compound this with the concept of the self-fulfilling prophecy and you have a no-win situation regarding self-esteem and successful strategies for stress management.

We all have many positive attributes, those qualities that we take pride in, from our physical, mental, emotional, and spiritual makeup. We need to be reminded of these qualities to boost our self-esteem when the gray clouds of life start to collect over our heads. Take a moment to reflect on your positive attributes: those qualities that make you unique. Select from all areas of your total wellbeing, including your physical, intellectual, emotional, and spiritual dimensions. Write them in a list, perhaps even describing each one and telling why you consider it to be an asset. If you can't come up with at least ten, ask a few friends to describe what they see as your positive attributes. You may be surprised to find what they see in you that you fail to recognize in yourself. On days when you need to boost your self-esteem, refer to this list.

26

UNWRITTEN LETTERS
A RESOLUTION PROCESS

Many times we wish to communicate with someone we love, like, or just know well, but for one reason or another—whether it be anger, procrastination or not finding the right words at the right time—we part ways without fully resolving those special feelings. There was once a college student whose former boyfriend took his life. In the note left behind, he specifically mentioned her, and the words haunted her for what seemed like an eternity. As a result of counseling, she decided to write him a letter to express her feelings of anger, sorrow, loneliness, and love. Through her words, her letter began the resolution process and ultimately her path toward inner peace.

This theme of resolution through letter writing has been the subject of many books, plays, and movies. In a movie made for television entitled *Message to my Daughter*, a young mother with a newborn baby discovers she has terminal cancer. As a part of her resolution process, she records several cassette tapes with personal messages to her daughter. Many father-son relationships also fall into this category, when emotional distance becomes a nearly impassable abyss. It is a common theme.

It has been said that with recent advances in technology, from the cellular telephone to the microchip, Americans are writing fewer and fewer personal letters. Sociologists worry that future generations will look back on this time period, the information high-tech age, and never really know what individuals were actually feeling and thinking because there will be few, if any, written entries to trace these perceptions. Moreover, psychologists agree that many of today's patients are troubled and unable to articulate their thoughts and feelings completely, which leaves them with feelings of unresolved stress.

This journal entry concerns the theme of resolution. The following are some suggestions that might inspire you to draft a letter to someone you have been meaning to write. Now is your chance.

1. Compose a letter to someone you were close to who has passed away or someone you haven't been in contact with for a long time. Tell that person what you have been up to, perhaps any major changes in your life, or changes that you foresee occurring in the months or years ahead. If you have any unresolved feelings toward this person, try expressing them in appropriately crafted words so that you can resolve these feelings and come to a sense of lasting peace.

2. Write a letter to yourself. Imagine that you have one month to live. What would you do in these last thirty days? Assume that there are no limitations. Whom would you see? Where would you visit? What would you do? Why?

3. Pretend that you now have a baby. What would you like to share with your son or daughter now, should, for some reason, you not have the opportunity to do so later in life? What would you like your child to know about you? For example, perhaps you would share things that you wanted to know about your parents or grandparents, which now are pieces missing in your life.

4. Write a letter to anyone you wish for whatever reason.

27

A LOG CABIN EXPERIENCE
CREATIVE WRITING

For many people, a log cabin tucked away in the mountains exudes romance and freedom: a communal spell with nature, a chance to leave life's drudgeries behind, a time to nurture the soul, rejuvenate the human spirit, and even clean out the cobwebs of the mind. At the turn of the nineteenth century, many mountain cabins were built for such escapes. Often the cabins contained a log book where visitors could share a word or two, such as a memorable experience or even a story for future cabin guests, and could be entertained with the exploits and stories of previous cabin visitors.

The chance for solitude high in the mountains often stimulates creative expression. Creative writing can be a healthy expression of thoughts, ideas, and feelings through the eyes of another character, in the third person voice or the first person in a new time period. Close your eyes for a moment and imagine you are sitting by the stone hearth in front of a large, glowing fire under a huge rack of deer antlers. Smell the pitch of the pine as it sparks and crackles in the fire. See the shadows of the fire dance on the log cabin walls, and feel the warmth of the lambskin rug underneath you as you sip a cup of hot tea or coffee. Imagine now, that it is your turn to write an entry in the cabin's visitors' log. What creative story do you have to pass along in these pages?

L. CARDAGNA
7/31/04
MIRABELLE AT BEAVER CREEK

28

THE THINGS I TAKE
FOR GRANTED

Almost instinctively, human beings have given thanks since they first set foot on earth. From animal sacrifices to banquet feasts to silent moments of praise, the occasion to show appreciation for the smallest of gifts to some of life's greatest pleasures is very much a part of the human condition. A unique tradition was established on the shores of the New World several hundred years ago when English immigrants and native Americans sat down to perhaps the most famous autumn feast ever created, Thanksgiving, and appropriately thereafter it became a yearly event.

It is easy to give thanks and praise in times of joy and happiness. It is rarely thought of, however, in times of crisis. Actually, stress can produce some very ungrateful attitudes. Stressful events tend to cloud the mind with thoughts of frustration and anguish, some directed inward, most directed outward, and these can leave little room for much else. When the Pilgrims sat down to the first turkey dinner, times were hard. There was no indoor plumbing; there were no drug stores, no credit cards, and no daycare centers. Life was a real challenge. But in that challenge, life was reduced to the simplest of terms. The challenge was survival. In our day and age, survival is pretty much a given. The question isn't "Will I survive?" but rather "How well can I live?" Although theoretically, the high-tech age has improved the quality of life, it also seems to drag with it the pressures that negate this standard of quality.

More stress and less time to enjoy life's simple pleasures can often make it difficult to take adequate time to sit back every now and then and appreciate the little things that make life special. Stress can act as blinders to our field of vision. By consciously taking these blinders off, we can see the whole picture in better focus. Taking things for granted is as much a part of human nature as giving thanks. But so often we don't know what we've got until it's gone. A list of things that you take for granted could be endless. But if you were to stop and think for a moment about what some of these might include, just what would they be and why?

29

WORDS FROM A SONG
REFLECTIONS ON PERSONAL RELATIONSHIPS

Have you ever heard a song, and after listening to the lyrics, thought to yourself, "I know somebody who really needs to hear these words"? In fact, you may actually feel like buying the cassette tape or compact disc and mailing it to that person with an anonymous note saying, "Drop what you're doing right now, sit and listen to the words of this song and reflect on its meaning."

We have all felt like this at some point in our lives. Sometimes it seems as though poets and song writers corner the market on the expression of thoughts and feelings. Given the chance, we might do as good a job ourselves. But there appears to be a mental passage in which words travel more accessibly when a melody accompanies them. The message really can connect with the soul. Here are the facts: relationships are tough to initiate, hard work to maintain, and, let's face it, there's no graceful way in which they can end. Through it all, communication is essential and sometimes words we hear in a song convey the message best.

Let us turn the tables for a moment. Pretend that someone you know sent you the words to a song and asked you to reflect on the song's meaning as it relates to you and the respective relationship. The following songs were selected to represent a variety of relationships: girlfriend, boyfriend, parental, and inner-self relationships. If you know these songs and have the lyrics at hand, select one and read the words and ponder their message. Then write down your thoughts as they come to mind. Should you have a favorite song lyric that might better serve this purpose, please feel free to write it down and then reflect on it.

SELECTED SONGS
"The Stranger," Billy Joel (*self-relationship*)
"Hasten Down the Wind," Warren Zevon (*girlfriend relationship*)
"Thinking of Leaving," Cheryl Wheeler (*divorce, parental relationship*)
"The Greatest Love of All," M. Masser and L. Creed (*self-relationship*)
"You Don't Know Me," Eddie Arnold (*boyfriend/girlfriend relationship*)
"If He's Ever Near," Karla Bonoff (*boyfriend relationship*)
"Father and Son," Cat Stevens (*parental relationship*)

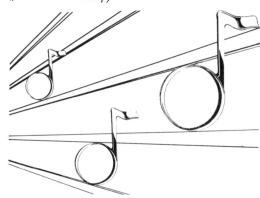

30

BRIDGING THE HEMISPHERES OF THOUGHT

In 1956 a researcher named Roger Sperry conducted some experiments on a handful of patients with grand mal epileptic seizures. In the procedure he created, he cut the corpus callosum, the bridge of neural fibers that connects the right and left hemispheres of the brain. Not only did the operation reduce the number and intensity of the grand mal seizures, it soon gave credence to a whole new concept of how the mind, through the brain, processes information. Roger Sperry's research led to a Nobel Prize in medicine and to the household expressions *right-* and *left-brain thinking*.

Western culture grooms and rewards left-brain thinking. And it is fair to say that judgmental thinking is one of our predominant traits. While it is true that the Western culture is left-brain dominant in thinking skills, the truth of the matter is that to be dominant in one style of thinking may actually be considered lopsided and imbalanced.

Here are some thinking skills allied with the left and right hemispheres of the brain, respectively: left-brain skills are associated with judgment, analysis, mathematical and verbal acuity, linear thought progression, and time consciousness; right-brain functioning is associated with global thinking, holistic thinking, imagination, humor, emotionality, spatial orientation, receptivity, and intuition.

1. How would you describe your dominant thinking style? Would you say that your left brain or right brain dominates?

2. If you were to make a guess or assumption as to why your thinking skills gravitate toward one direction or the other, what would be your explanation?

3. One of the basic themes of wellness is balance—in this case, balance of the right-brain and left-brain functions. Based on your answer to the first question, what are your dominant thinking skills and your nondominant thinking skills? What are some ways you can balance your patterns by bridging between the right and left hemispheres of your brain?

31

EMOTIONAL WELLBEING

Emotional wellbeing is best described as "the ability to feel and express the entire range of human emotions and to control them, not be controlled by them." Sounds like a pretty tall order, huh? Well, it doesn't have to be.

What is the range of human emotions? Everything from anger to love, and all that's in between. No emotion is excluded, meaning it is perfectly all right to feel angry, jealous, giddy, sad, depressed, light-hearted, and silly. All of these feelings comprise the total human experience.

A well-accepted theory suggests that early in our development we spend the greatest amount of time trying on and exploring emotions. But if you are like most people, you were told at an early age, "Wipe that smile off your face," "Big boys don't cry," "Don't you ever talk back to me," or "I'll give you something to cry about." Perhaps our parents had good intentions, or perhaps they were just at wit's end. Regardless of what prompts such comments, most youngsters interpret the message altogether differently than intended. Instead of relating only to the moment, most children take the meaning of such messages globally and think it is never OK to laugh or to cry.

If we hear these messages enough, we begin to deny some of our feelings by stuffing them down into our unconscious minds, only to meet them head-on later in life.

The second half of the emotional wellbeing equation says that to be emotionally well we must control our feelings, not let them control us. Our feelings do control us when we refuse to feel and express them or when we linger too long in the moods of anger, anxiety, depression, grief, or boredom. The result is stagnation, not dynamic living.

Here are some questions to ponder about your own sense of emotional wellbeing:

1. What is your least favorite emotion, one that you don't like to feel or perhaps would rather avoid feeling? Can you explain why?

2. Combing your memory, can you remember a time (or times) when you were told not to act or feel a certain way (e.g., "Big boys don't cry")? Take a moment to describe this incident.

3. What is your favorite emotion? Why? How often would you say you feel this throughout the day?

4. If you feel you may be the kind of person who doesn't acknowledge or express your emotions, can you think of a way (or ways) to change your behavior and begin to gain a sense of emotional balance?

32

MENTAL WELLBEING

Mental wellbeing is defined as "the ability to gather, process, recall, and communicate information." If this sounds a bit similar to a how a computer works, there's a good reason. The personal computer is closely based on the functioning processes of the mind.

There is one aspect of life that can compromise our ability to gather, process, recall, and communicate information: stress. Stress occurs when we are overwhelmed with sensory stimulation. In essence, our circuits are overloaded. In computer language, the system is down.

Although the mind needs time to clear itself of thoughts when the circuits are overloaded, it also craves stimulation. Mental wellbeing is that point of balance where stimulation equals clarity.

With this definition in mind, what do you do to help clear the mind when you are feeling overwhelmed? (By´ the way, journal writing is an excellent way to do this). Learning to cleanse the mind is essential when you are in college because then, unlike at any other time in your life, you are constantly being flooded with information to gather, process, recall, and communicate from your course work.

Equally important is what you do to stimulate your mind. As the expression goes, man does not live by bread alone, nor do college students live by lectures, textbooks, and class work. Books for leisure, magazines, the internet, the discovery channel, and museums are just a few ways to seek additional stimulation. What do you do to achieve this balance?

33

COMPASSION IN ACTION

Love and compassion are necessities, not luxuries. Without them, humanity cannot survive.
With them, we can make a joint effort to solve the problems of the whole humankind.
The Dalai Lama

Several years ago an expression appeared all over the country, on bumper stickers, billboards, napkins, and T-shirts; it read "Practice random kindness and senseless acts of beauty." Its creator, Anne Herbert, wanted to send a message to people about the importance of compassion in action. The news headlines rarely speak of this aspect of humanity. Rather, they tend to focus on all the negative aspects of life. It didn't take long for Herbert's message to change the focus of people's attention toward the brighter side of life. People began to put love into action by being more polite and showing more signs of altruism, and some of these stories did make the news.

Compassion in action is another way to describe service, and service can come about in many ways. Compassion in action is perhaps the epitome of unconditional love, where nothing is expected in return. Acts such as these are done without expectations or rewards. Anonymous gifts and exchanges are often signs of compassion in action. Putting a quarter in an expired parking meter and giving up a seat on a plane so a husband and wife can sit next to each other are two examples of what Anne Herbert meant when she wrote "Practice random kindness and senseless acts of beauty."

There are those who say we are put here on this planet with a unique capacity to love. Love isn't just a theory. For love to be real, it must be put into action. Compassion comes in many forms, but pity isn't one of them, as pity is fear-based thinking. There is no room for fear in compassion.

Sometimes when we are stressed, the last thing we want to do is be of service to others. Giving of ourselves in times of need, however, brings back that which we need ourselves many times over—love!

On the next page, please list twelve ways you can be of service, practice random acts of kindness, or put your compassion in action. After you create this list, begin to put your thoughts into action.

1.

2.

3.

4.

5.

6.

7.

8.

9.

10.

11.

12.

34

HEALTHY LOCUS OF CONTROL

Several decades ago a psychologist named Julian Rotter had an idea that went like this. There are two human drives: internal and external motivation, or as Dr. Rotter called them, an internal and external locus of control.

People who have an external locus of control are those who tend to feel as though their lives are controlled by outside factors such as the weather, the stars, the government, destiny, and influences beyond their own domain. A person with an extreme locus of control is someone who in essence places blame (or credit) on someone or something else for his or her misfortunes (or blessings). People who fall into this category more likely than not see themselves as passive participants in the game of life. An internal locus of control signifies a vantage point where individuals see the responsibility as residing within themselves. They rely on their own strengths and inner resources. When faced with a problem or difficult situation, people with an internal locus of control stand up to adversity by themselves. They see themselves as having an active, not passive, role in their lives.

Most likely there are few people who epitomize either end of the spectrum, but we tend to gravitate toward one side or the other. In terms of health, a person with an external locus of control would blame a cold, headache, ulcer, or heart attack on somebody or something. Conversely, a person with an internal locus of control would assume responsibility for his or her own health, and as long as there is no guilt associated with it, this is something health care professionals encourage.

Where do you see yourself on this continuum? Do you see yourself with an internal or external locus of control? Are you someone who is easily motivated by trophies, medals, and horoscopes or does your source of inspiration come primarily from within? Take a few minutes to ponder the concept of a healthy locus of control and share your thoughts here.

35

FREEDOM AND RESPONSIBILITY

It's a pity that the word responsibility wasn't included with the phrase, "life, liberty, and the pursuit of happiness." Perhaps the idea of responsibility was so obviously part of the concept of freedom that it only had to be implied. We may never know, but often what is implied on one day is ignored or forgotten on the next. Such is the case with the concept of responsibility.

Freedom, or liberty, is one of the cornerstones of the American culture. Responsibility should be too. In truth, you cannot have one without the other. Each serves as a check and balance for the other. Psychologist Viktor Frankl once said that if we have a Statue of Liberty on the East Coast we should have a Statue of Responsibility on the West Coast to provide balance to the human race.

When we first leave home and head off to college, we assert our independence with various freedoms that we didn't have access to under the rule of our parents. We may stay out later, we may sleep in later—actually we may do a whole host of things that we would never dream of doing at home. Freedom to do what we please is wonderful. But the flip side to freedom is responsibility, for ultimately we are responsible for our every act, even if the apparent consequences seem too distant to think about.

Such is the case with many reckless health behaviors (e.g. drinking, drugs, irresponsible sex). When we are young, our youth seems to act as a form of immortality, yet the illusion is a short-lived one, for every act of freedom holds with it a consequence of responsibility. In actuality, freedom does not act in opposition to responsibility but in collaboration with it.

Now is the time to ask yourself about your freedoms, your health behaviors, and your sense of responsibility about them. Please describe your feelings about these two values and how they impact on your choice of health behaviors.

36

BOUNDARIES AND BARRIERS

Ego boundaries must be hardened before they can be softened.
M. Scott Peck

There is a part of the human condition that begs for boundaries, and we learn this at an early age. "That's mine," we say. "You cannot have that." As we get older, boundaries contain the parameters of our lives, and they are made manifest by our property and the rules and guidelines we establish to help govern our lives. Like other members of the animal kingdom, we mark and stake our territory and then spend the better part of our lives defending it. Granted, there are times when we tread across other people's boundaries and there are times when feel our space is invaded by others. Each time boundaries are violated, we feel threatened, and stress ensues.

The violation of boundaries is a significant stressor to many people. Although boundaries can be trespassed under any circumstance, boundary violations happen most frequently through the involvement of intimate relationships, where love gives way to dominance and control. As the expression goes, "The reason you start a relationship isn't the reason you stay in it." In an effort to please a significant other, we relax our boundaries. The result is an invitation to enter; however, eventually boundaries must be reestablished. This is where problems arise. Inevitably, boundaries need to be reestablished. If the other person chooses not to leave, tension will certainly arise and feelings of victimization will ensue. For example, she would prefer not to get intimate; he forces himself upon her. She asks him not to call after 11 p.m.; he frequently calls after midnight. He asks not to be called at work; she calls four to five times a day. The majority of problems in intimate relationships come down to boundary issues and boundary violations. Each deals with the issue of control. As an adult, defending your boundaries requires assertiveness, not aggression.

This journal theme asks you to look at boundaries from two vantage points: your own and those of significant people in your life. First, what are your boundaries? How aware are you of the parameters you have established in your life to help guide you through the course of your life and maintain a sense of control? If you are not sure of what your boundaries are, begin to identify the rules and guidelines you have established for yourself, such as the time you go to bed, how late you take phone calls, when it's appropriate for people to visit, or when you decide to treat someone to lunch or dinner.

Next, ask yourself how often you feel your boundaries are violated and by whom.

After you have looked at boundaries from inside the comfort of your mind, take a look at those people whose lives are intertwined with your own: friends, husband, wife, significant other, parents, children, co-workers and perhaps even your boss. Now let's turn the tables for a moment. Are you a boundary violator?

37

ROLE MODELS AND HEROES

Everything I do and say with anyone makes a difference.
Gita Bellen

It has been said that since the advent of television and video technology, the culture of American heroes has changed significantly, if it has not disappeared altogether. In the late 1980s a popular weekly magazine conducted a survey identifying current American heroes. It showed that the top twenty-five people selected were either movie stars, television actors, or rock musicians. Today people are still fascinated with celebrities' ideals of fame and fortune.

In days gone by there was a different fascination that created legends, catapulted individuals to hero status, and inspired people to follow in their footsteps. The early American heroes and role models were the inventors, the explorers, the philosophers, and the movers and shakers of the world, for example, Ben Franklin, Florence Nightingale, Babe Ruth, Booker T. Washington, Mark Twain, Lewis and Clark, Amelia Earhart, Carl Jung, Abraham Lincoln, Eleanor Roosevelt, Charles Lindbergh, Thomas Edison, Harriet Tubman, Henry David Thoreau, Rosa Parks, and John Glenn.

It's quite well known that we all are capable of heroic deeds and there are a great many unrecognized heroes currently in our midsts. These are just ordinary people who do extraordinary things, people who give 100 percent effort against insurmountable odds and come out on top. If you were to ask a child who his or her hero is, you might likely hear the reply "Mom" or "Dad." In the course of a lifetime, however, a great many people influence us; some we never meet but perhaps only hear or read about.

When you stop to think about it, some people can have a profound positive influence on our lives—perhaps more than we recognize. The following questions are provided as food for thought regarding your role models and life heroes.

1. What person would you say has had the greatest influence on your life? Why?

2. Most people model their adult behavior and even thoughts/perceptions as a result of a synthesis of several people and the influence they have had. What people do you admire and tend to model some of your thoughts and behaviors on?

3. If you could have lunch with anyone—living or dead—just once, who would you like to break bread with and tap into for an hour, and why?

4. We not only have role models and heroes, but we are role models. We not only absorb the light, but we also reflect it. Who in your life have you been a role model for? Whom have you touched, inspired, and reflected light toward?

38

ONE PERSONAL WISH

Aladdin had three and Pinocchio had one with a rebate. Hardly a day goes by that we don't wish for something. From birthday cake candles to Thanksgiving dinner wishbones, the wish is as much a part of American culture as apple pie and baseball. In the Orient wise men are occasionally heard telling young children the Chinese curse "May all your wishes come true." Likewise, Oscar Wilde once said, "When the Gods want to punish you, they answer your prayers." When wishes are based on greed, trouble undoubtedly lies ahead. But often wishes can be the seeds of creativity, and creativity can have a host of wonderful events and possibilities.

Wishes consist of one part hope, one part love, and one part sweat. Although the fulfillment of our wishes, prayers, and dreams may take longer than we would like, wishes can come true. Fairy tales aside, if you were to be granted one personal wish, what would it be and, perhaps most importantly, why?

39

CONTROL
A DOUBLE-EDGED SWORD

"God, grant me the serenity to accept the things I cannot change, the courage to change the things I can, and the wisdom to know the difference." "The Serenity Prayer," by Reinhold Neibuhr, embodies one of the cornerstone principles of the recovery program, initiated through Alcoholics Anonymous.

The unyielding message of the prayer is about control. Control is a paradox. It can be perceived as either good or bad. For this reason, it can be compared to a double-edged sword. To master this tool and not inflict self-damage one must understand and recognize what one does and does not have control over and have the wisdom to know the difference. Many people use control as manipulative behavior. Often they try to control others and events because they find these easier to control than their own thoughts and actions. People who employ manipulative behavior mistake control for responsibility. This manipulative behavior can become addictive. Each episode of control is like the next "fix"—a false inflation of one's self-worth until the next controllable opportunity. The result can be a vicious circle, and it can be a very unhealthy behavior. Conversely, control is also said to be one of three prime characteristics (in conjunction with challenge and commitment) in what psychologists now refer to as the *hardy personality* or *stress-resistant personality.* Unlike manipulative behavior, this perspective focuses on self-control as a function of willpower.

Are you a master swordsman with a strong sense of self-control, or does the action of manipulative behavior metaphorically cut and nick your hands? Do people and events that you seem to have no control over frustrate you? Do you spend a lot of energy against the flow, managing events that you feel only you can do well? Do you mistake or have you mistaken responsibility for control? How is your sense of willpower? And finally, what are some ways you can become a master swordsman with the power of self-control?

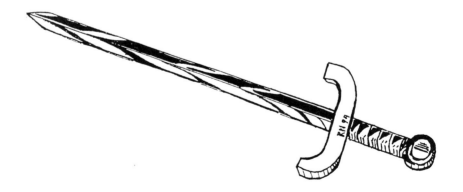

40

CONVERSATIONS WITH GOD

How come when we talk to God, it's called praying,
but when God talks to us, it's called schizophrenia?
Lily Tomlin

Recently there has been much interest in the topics of spirituality, angels, miracles, and the healing power of prayer. It could be said that we in the American culture are going through a spiritual renaissance. What's the reason, you ask? One reason may be that after decades of materialistic pleasures, a large percentage of the baby boom generation as well as members of the so-called Generation X are feeling a lack of personal satisfaction. In essence, the connection made to material possessions has placed a wedge between a person and his or her divine self. So we find ourselves in a time of much spiritual hunger.

It is important to remember that although there is a clear distinction between the concepts of spiritually and religion ("spirituality connects, whereas religions divide and separate," in the words of a famous conductor), there is virtually no difference between spiritual and divine things. Granted, even though everyone's idea of God is different, this really makes no difference; it's only important that you feel comfortable with your perceptions. Regardless of your conceptions, perceptions, beliefs and attitudes, conversation with God is at some level the same as talking with your higher self. You might call this prayer.

Larry Dossey has spent several years researching the concept of prayer. Like others before him who have tried to understand the divine nature of humanity, he has come to the realization that a prayer is merely a thought directed toward a power or energy that lies outside the domain of the five senses.

Although several religions introduce the concept of prayer as a memorization of an incantation (e.g., The Lord's Prayer or the Hail Mary) to be said in times of want or distress, this is just one of a host of different ways to reach and speak to the God source that resides in and permeates all things. Prayer need not only be said in times of stress. This form of communication can be offered in times of joy as well. Perhaps most importantly, prayer is an ongoing dialogue with your own thoughts, giving the opportunity to elevate your level of consciousness by realizing your connectedness to all things. So in actuality, all thought has prayer potential.

Prayer is also a reflection of your relationship with that part of you that is divine. This journal theme asks you to reflect on this aspect of your health and to continue the dialogue on paper.

41

THE CHILD WITHIN

To see a universe of life in a few blades of grass while lying face down on a lawn under the summer sun. To catch yourself laughing at the silliest idea or crying with remorse without any inhibition to stop. To believe in the power of magic and be suspended in time with curiosity. To see life as an adventure and be swept away in the colors of a rainbow to a faraway land. To love without conditions. These are the precious moments of childhood. Conversely, childhood can be filled with many dark and lonely moments as well: battles of sibling rivalry, abusive parents, ridicule from our peers, and unending hours of loneliness. At times, childhood can be filled with both glorious naiveté and painful abandonment. Some of these aspects of our youth fade too quickly as the seasons of our life spin faster and faster toward adulthood, while others linger on with many unresolved feelings.

Despite the maturation process into our adult years, within each of us there still remains a child who continually needs to be nurtured, loved, and protected. Let's pretend for a moment that you could actually meet a younger version of yourself who is four to five years old. Behind the ruffled hair, wide eyes, and missing tooth is a child longing to be loved and begging for acceptance. With years, even decades of experience behind you now, what would you say to this child? What could you say to comfort, love, or nurture this child within you? Ponder for a moment some comforting words of advice, some thoughts of love that you might like to have heard at that age to help you in the transition into your adolescence and adulthood.

Also, as with any good conversation, there is dialogue from both sides. Listen closely to the child within and discuss what he or she is begging to tell you. Perhaps your inner child will suggest that it has been too long since you lay face down on a summer lawn under the sun and explored blades of grass. Perhaps he or she will tell you that it's okay to cry or laugh out loud again or to explore your sense of creativity and curiosity. We have much to learn from the child within us. Share the thoughts of this conversation with your younger self.

42

THE GARDEN OF EDEN

Sigmund Freud is credited with saying that the average adult thinks about sex every thirty seconds. While the time interval may vary from person to person, there's no doubt that our sexual drive, along with our drive for nourishment and sleep, is an important part of our daily makeup. Consequently, the sexual drive can contribute to much frustration and stress. Regardless of gender, individuals become sexually conscious during puberty, around the ages of eleven to thirteen. It is not until people reach adulthood at the age of eighteen that their sexual behavior is fully recognized and accepted. Between puberty and adulthood there exists a five-to nine-year period of potential personal frustration.

Social, cultural, and religious mores and expectations only confound this issue with rules, laws, and dogma linking the approval of sexual activity with marriage. What can be really confusing are all the mixed messages from the media and advertising industry that are loaded with sexual overtones and innuendoes. Moreover, there are many issues and concerns adding to this frustration, including unplanned pregnancy, sexually transmitted diseases, rejection, birth control and contraception, value conflicts, date rape, homosexuality, and guilt. Later in the life cycle, more issues arise that are related to sex anxiety, including inability to conceive, low sperm count, sexual addiction, impotency, sexual inactivity, and sexual dissatisfaction. This list goes on and on.

Unlike our other drives, the human sexual drive carries the heavy burden of incredible responsibility. As a result, the implications surrounding sexuality can be very stressful. Without a doubt, good communication is a crucial factor in reducing some of the anxiety regarding human sexuality, but we must initiate much of the communication ourselves, to ourselves, and from there to those with whom we are intimately involved. Now is a good time to initiate this communication with yourself. Is sexuality a current stressor in your life? Take a moment to do some soul-searching on this issue.

43

VICTIMHOOD

God, grant me the serenity to accept the things I cannot change,
the courage to change the things I can, and the wisdom to know the difference.
Reinhold Neibuhr

The headlines read: Man sues fast-food chain because coffee is *too hot*. Woman sues airline for missing flight to wedding. Lawyer of defendant sues lawyer of plaintiff. The United States has more lawyers per capita than any other country in the world. We live in a litigious society where blame is constantly placed on somebody else and lawsuits are common. Everyone is suing everyone. Psychologists have another name for this phenomenon: victimhood.

It is easy to blame someone else when things don't go our way. When expectations go unmet, whether it is coffee that burns our tongue or a delayed airline flight, we can easily feel violated. If left unchecked, these feelings of violation can quickly turn to victimization, and revenge seems to be the only solution. And the greater the emotional damage, the greater the penalty we wish to inflict on those who we feel have wronged us.

It is fair to say that victimhood in America is at an all-time high, as citizens repeatedly experience unmet expectations. A general feeling of frustration is the precursor to victimhood. At some point, though, we need to realize that we are not passive victims in the game of life. We have an active role in every situation we encounter. There are some things we can control, and there are many we cannot. As the Serenity Prayer suggests, it is wise to know the difference! Moreover, we need to learn to take responsibility, not only for our actions, but also for our feelings.

Is there something you have felt victimized about lately? Grades, term papers, flat tires, or delayed flights? If you have, you're not alone. But take a moment to look at whatever makes you feel victimized right now. Describe the situation as you see it, as you experienced it. Then try to describe it as objectively as possible. Feelings of victimization are often associated with feelings of anger. Can you recognize any feelings of anger when you sense a moment of victimization? Why do you feel this way? Are you one who is prone to feelings of victimization? Why do you suppose this is so? Knowing the relationship between anger and victimization, can you begin to outline ways in which you can work toward resolving these feelings and perhaps toward acknowledging a greater part in the responsibility of those events in your life, including acceptance of those things you cannot change?

44

ENERGY: THE LIFE FORCE

Look, and it cannot be seen. Listen, and it cannot be heard.
Form that includes all forms. Subtle beyond all conception.
Lao Tzu

There is a life force of subtle energy that surrounds and permeates us all. The Chinese call this force *chi*. To harmonize with the universe, to move in unison with this energy, to move as free as running water is to be at peace with or to be one with the universe. This harmony of energy promotes tranquillity and inner peace.

To understand the concept of chi, it is helpful to view it in the cultural perspective where it originated. Clinically speaking, the Chinese concept of health is quite different from that understood in the Western hemisphere. Unlike the Western concept of health as the absence of disease and illness produced by bacteria and viruses, health for the Chinese is an unrestricted current of subtle energy that runs throughout the body. When chi, the subtle energy that flows through the body in a network of meridians, or "energy gates," is restricted or congested, the body is susceptible to physiological dysfunction. Hence, disturbances within the human energy field will result in physical symptoms of disease or illness.

According to Chinese medicine, it is not necessarily the bacterium or virus that causes physical dysfunction or disease; these are thought to be present everywhere. Rather, a state of poor health is thought to result from both internal and external factors that ultimately do one in because of low resistance from nonharmonious (blocked) energy. Stated another way, these "pathogens" are constantly present; it is low resistance to them that makes one vulnerable to the disease. From a Chinese perspective, an unrestricted flow of energy helps maintain one's resistance to disturbing influences, be they biological, psychological, or sociological in nature.

Let's assume for a moment that the Chinese philosophy of health holds some merit, that a person's health status is based on the flow of energy. Perhaps you can gain a new perspective on your health by sensing your own energy levels. The following questions ask you to examine your energy level(s) as the basis for your health status.

1. What do you notice about your level of energy and your health status? For example, are there times when your energy is low, and then you catch a cold or flu? Describe what you feel like when you are energized and compare it to when you feel drained of energy.

2. Do certain circumstances, events, or episodes seem to drain your energy? What are they? Do you see patterns here?

3. When you are feeling rundown, as if you are running on empty, what do you do to recharge yourself?

4. In the Chinese culture, T'ai chi, acupuncture, and acupressure are used to equilibrate the body's energy levels, clear the meridians, and restore one to a sense of wellbeing. Have you tried one or more of these techniques? If so, what are your impressions? If not, would you consider giving one of them a try?

45

HEALTHY PLEASURES

In the book *Healthy Pleasures*, authors Robert Ornstein and David Sobel recommend that, in order to create a sense of balance in our lives, we should remember to pat ourselves on the back, take responsibility for our moments of happiness, and engage in a host of behaviors that bring a sense of joy and satisfaction to our lives.

Now you may say, "Hey, I already do this!" But by and large, most people don't, especially after they get out of college and get caught up in making money, paying bills, raising kids, and taking care of parents.

Healthy pleasures are just that—healthy. They don't cost much either. To look at a sunset, to take an early morning walk in the woods, to treat yourself to an ice cream cone—these are healthy pleasures. How quickly they are forgotten when our world seems stressed!

This journal entry asks you to list twenty-five healthy pleasures that you participate in on a regular basis. If you cannot come up with twenty-five, then list some healthy pleasures that you intend to do soon.

1. _____

2. _____

3. _____

4. _____

5. _____

6. _____

7. _____

8. _____

9. _____

10. _____

11. _____

12. _____

13. _____

14. _____

15. _____

16. _____

17. _____

18. _____

19. _____

20. _____

21. _____

22. _____

23. _____

24. _____

25. _____

46

SPIRITUAL WELLBEING

Human spirituality is so complex that it seems to defy an adequate definition or description. It is often compared to love, self-esteem, faith, and so many human characteristics that seem to be related to it. This we do know: Human spirituality involves a strong self-relationship as well as connectedness, or strong relationships with others, a strong personal value system, and a meaningful purpose in life. Unlike religions that have integrated these components, human spirituality has no rules, no dogma, and no set agenda. These concepts are related but separate entities. Psychologist Carl Jung once said, "Every crisis over the age of thirty is spiritual in nature." There is a definite relationship between stress and spirituality.

Over the years, M. Scott Peck, author of *The Road Less Traveled*, has studied the concepts of human spirituality, and he has developed a four-stage model to understand spiritual development. Each stage has many layers; and indeed, some people seem to hover somewhere between stages. Be that as it may, these categories can help us to focus on our spiritual path.

1. **Chaotic/antisocial:** At this stage a person is manipulative, unprincipled, and governed by selfish pleasure under spiritual bankruptcy. His or her lifestyle is unorganized, in chaos or crisis, and headed for the rocks, which in turn causes much pain. All blame is externalized and projected on others.

2. **Formal/institutional:** At this stage a sudden conversion occurs where a person finds shelter in an institution (prison, military, or church) for security, structure, rules, and guidance. People in this stage see God as a loving but punitive figure, an "Irish cop in the sky." God is personified with human characteristics (a human face, a masculine pronoun, *He, His, etc.*). Institutions do, however, make some order out of the chaos.

3. **Skeptic/individual:** At this stage the person, while searching for answers, rejects the institution that claims to have them. He or she is a "born-again atheist," a person who no longer buys into the system of rules and dogma but still believes there is something out there and wants to find it. According to Peck, this is a crucial stage of development.

4. **Mystical/Communal:** The most mature stage, when someone actively searches for new answers to life's age-old questions but feels comfortable knowing that he or she may never find the answers. A person's vision of God at this stage is as internal as it is external. Additionally, such an individual sees the need for community, or bonding, and tries to foster this. Finally, those who reach this stage realize that it is only the beginning.

Most importantly, spiritual wellbeing is an unfolding, an evolution of higher consciousness. Spirituality is also very personal; we each travel on our path at our own pace.

1. How would you define spirituality?
2. What state of wellbeing is your human spirit currently in?
3. In what stage of development in Peck's model do you see yourself?
4. Is your perception of God personified? Please explain.
5. Do you have a relationship with God? If so, how strong or weak is it? What steps could you take to improve this relationship?

47

POSITIVE AFFIRMATION STATEMENTS

Positive affirmation statements are thoughts or expressions that you can repeat to yourself to boost your self-esteem. These words of inspiration highlight the positive aspects of your own personality traits and characteristics that enhance and nurture your self-esteem. They are expressions that build confidence, provide inspiration, lift the spirit to rise above mediocrity and help you function at your highest human potential.

It is easy to give yourself negative feedback about almost anything. We each have a critic who metaphorically sits on our shoulder and whispers negative thoughts in our ear. The media does this too, striking at our insecurities through subliminal and overt advertising with over 1,500 messages per day. In addition, we often interpret feedback to be negative from family, friends, and other people who pass in and out of our lives. But worst of all, perhaps as a learned behavior, we continually feed ourselves negative thoughts, which continually deflate self-esteem.

The use of positive affirmation statements is really a behavior modification technique used in conjunction with relaxation techniques (deep breathing or mental imagery) to train the mind to give the battered ego positive strokes, and strengthen self-esteem. Although there are no specific rules, there are some guidelines that can make these positive affirmations work for you. (1) Phrase your affirmation in the present tense, such as "I am a lovable person." (2) Phrase your affirmation in the most positive way. (3) Make your affirmation simple, clear, and precise. (4) Choose an affirmation that feels right for you.

The following is a sample of some positive affirmation statements that others have used for this purpose. A positive affirmation statement should be a personal thought or expression. However, if you cannot think of one right away, feel free to use one or more of these. Eventually, you may want to take a moment to think of one that is personal. Positive affirmation statements should be somewhat short— something you can repeat to yourself in one breath.

1. Damn, I'm good.
2. I am one with the Tao.
3. Love is the answer.
4. I am calm and relaxed.
5. I have confidence in myself.
6. I am an important piece of the whole.
7. I am a lovable person.
8. I radiate success!
9. I am worthy of being loved.
10. I am the source of my happiness and security.

Now that you have chosen your positive affirmation statement, write down fifteen places or times of day that you can say this to yourself to reinforce this message. Then, do it!

48

EMBRACE THE SHADOW

Have you ever noticed how often we judge other people and note their imperfections, especially when we feel violated or victimized by their actions? How often do you find fault with others who cross your path, or worse, become obstacles on it? And have you ever noticed how much easier it is to find fault with someone when you have a reason not to like him or her? Have you noticed that the easiest time to pass judgment is when you're most stressed? If you feel this way, you are not alone. And if you are like most people, you may find yourself pointing your finger at several people in the course of a day who *seem* to make your life miserable.

It has often been said that those flaws and foibles that we point out in others are merely reflections of our own imperfections. As a defense to protect our egos, we pass them off on others because it is painful to acknowledge them in our own being. Psychologist Carl Jung called this the *shadow*, the dark side of human nature that resides within each of us. It was Jung's belief that those who refuse to acknowledge their own shortcomings—their dark side—yet project them on others will constantly do battle with stress. Jung felt that we must not only acknowledge our dark side but come to terms with it—embrace it, if you will. For until it is acknowledged and "domesticated," we will never truly be at peace with ourselves.

So how do we learn to "embrace the shadow"? First, it is important to recognize that each human being has a shadow. Having done this, call to mind one or two people with whom you feel at odds, pinpoint what it is in these people that you dislike, despise, or distrust, and then write these characteristics down and explain why. Next, run a personal inventory on your thoughts and actions, the dark side of your personality, and see if there is some commonality with the individual(s) you just listed. Remember, where there is light there will always be a shadow, and having a dark side doesn't make you a bad person. Describe some ways that you can learn to embrace your shadow.

49

HUMOR IS THE BEST MEDICINE
THINGS THAT MAKE ME SMILE AND LAUGH

Life is full of absurdities, incongruities, and events that tickle our funny bone. For instance, Charlie Chaplin once got third place in a Charlie Chaplin look-alike contest. Since the day in 1964 when Norman Cousins checked out of a hospital room and into a hotel room across the street where he literally laughed his way back to health from a life-threatening disease, the medical world has stood up and taken notice. Humor really is good medicine.

Today, there is a whole new scientific discipline called *psychoneuroimmunology* (PNI), the study of the relationship between the mind and the body and the effects each has on the other. It is no secret that negative emotions (e.g., anger, fear, guilt, worry, depression, and loneliness) can have a detrimental effect on the body, manifesting into disease and illness. Although there is much to be understood, we now know that, just as negative emotions can have a negative effect on the body, positive emotions (e.g., joy, love, hope, and the feelings associated with humor) can have a positive effect on the body by speeding the healing process and promoting total wellbeing.

Humor is a great stress reducer. Humor acts as a coping mechanism to help us deal with life's hardships. It softens the walls of the ego, makes us feel less defensive, unmasks the naked truth in a comical way, and often gives us a clearer perspective and focus in our everyday lives. Comic relief is used in many stress management programs, hospitals, and work settings to reduce the effects of stress. Stress is often associated with negative attitudes that really deflate self-esteem. A preponderance of negative emotions can taint our view of the world around us, perpetuating the stress cycle. There has to be a balance! What researchers are now discovering is that we need to incorporate positive emotions to achieve this balance, and humor is one of the answers.

Although one could turn to the television to catch a few laughs, the greater the variety of humor vehicles (books, movies, live comedians, and music) one is exposed to, the more rewarding the riches. Sometimes all we have to do is dig through our memory to find a tickler.

1. How would you rate your sense of humor? Do you exercise it often? Do you exercise it correctly? Offensive humor (sarcasm, racist and sexist humor, and practical jokes) can actually promote stress. What are some ways to improve your sense of humor?

2. What is your favorite kind of humor (parody, slapstick, satire, black humor, nonsense, irony, puns)? What type of humor do you fall back on to reduce your stress?

3. What would you consider to be the funniest moment(s) of your life?

4. What are some of the funniest moments that you can recall from any situation that the mere thought of puts a grin or secret smile on your face?

5. In the song, "My Favorite Things," Julie Andrews sings about a host of things that flood her mind with joy and bring a smile to her face. What would your list include?

6. Make a list of things to do, places to go, and people to see to lift your spirits when the occasion calls for it.

50

PLAYING IN THE GARAGE

*Most large companies should remember
that they began with a person playing in the garage.*
Roger von Oech

Have you ever heard of the expression "Don't put all your eggs in one basket?" With regard to managing stress, this expression means to see yourself as more than a student and more than your job. If all your eggs are in the same basket and the basket drops, you are going to have a mess. Diversifying your interests protects you from having a bunch of broken eggs.

We are not just our job or our paycheck. We are so much more than that. Unfortunately the puritan ethic is still very influential in America, where the old adage "Work equals worth" undermines our best efforts to live a balanced life. If you assume that your life is your work then all your eggs are in the same basket, and a bad day is akin to the basket's being dropped and the emotional mess that ensues.

All work and no play is a recipe for stress. Play is part of the human equation. In today's rushed lifestyle, it is also a prescription for health. As children we are often told by our parents to go out and play, but we never quite hear that as adults. So how do adults play? Sometimes through sports and recreation but mostly through hobbies. Playing in the garage or basement invites us to pursue an interest that takes our minds off the stress of work. Hobbies can divert us from occupational stress. There is also another benefit. The creativity engaged in hobbies often transfers into other areas of our lives to help to resolve problems at home or work.

So what do you do for play? What are your hobbies? How often do you do them? If you don't have any hobbies, what interests can you pursue with greater ambition? Once you have made this list, discover how you can start (or restart) a hobby and put more play back into your life.

51

A TRAUMATIC EXPERIENCE

Into our lives a little rain must fall, but it seems that once or twice it becomes a devastating flood, and we subsequently get pulled under and washed away in the currents. Broken bones, the death of a close friend or loved one, and child abuse are just a handful of life's many tragedies. "Tragedy," it is said, "keeps a person humble." But it can also leave physical, mental, emotional, and spiritual scars that may take a lifetime to heal. Times like these are often referred to as "the dark nights of the soul."

Reactions may vary, but immediately after experiencing a tragedy, people sometimes talk nervously. This is one of the initial manifestations of grief. This stage is often followed by withdrawal and eventually by a slow reemergence into society. These types of experiences from years ago can affect our outlook and behavior on several issues, often without our knowledge. If you have been spared a personal tragedy, consider yourself lucky. If you have experienced an event of this nature and wish to recount it here, feel free to do so. Peace.

52

GOOD GRIEF!

Pain is inevitable. Suffering is optional.
M. Kathleen Casey

If you have ever read the comic strip *Peanuts*, you have probably seen Charlie Brown, Lucy, Linus, or Snoopy utter the words "Good grief." The expression may seem like an oxymoron. How can grief be good? The expression of grief arises from a loss, for example, of a parent, a lover, a spouse, a pet, or anyone or anything of major significance.

Grief is not just a human emotion. It is noted among most if not all animals. To feel and express grief is good; when it is not acknowledged and expressed, the residue can have a devastating effect on the body.

The most common sign of grief is the act of crying. Growing up you may have heard the expression "Stop crying." A little child infers that crying is not acceptable behavior. The consequence of this is that we don't learn to grieve properly. In later years our period of grieving can become rather extended, almost in an effort to make up for all the losses we didn't grieve for properly as children. So, the bottom line is that grieving is good. However, there are some caveats. Too brief a time of grieving may be denial of the loss. Excessive or prolonged grieving can lead to depression and thus be a major obstacle on the human journey, preventing you from getting on with your life.

Has there been a time when you were overcome with feelings of grief? What happened? By writing about it, you begin to bring closure to the grieving process if you are not already there.

Do you ever feel guilty about your feelings of grief? If so, can you trace these guilty feelings to a time or place when your grieving was halted with words like "Big boys don't cry" or "Aren't you over that yet?"?

This journal theme invites you to explore your grief, so feel free to add any comments you wish. Good grief! Go for it!

53

ARCHETYPES AND SYMBOLS

If the unconscious is anything at all,
it must consist of earlier evolutionary stages of our conscious psyche
Carl Gustav Jung

It is not uncommon to be asked several times in the course of our early lives, "What do you want to be when you grow up?" Some people are influenced by their parents to become doctors or lawyers. Others are inspired by their teachers. But is there something other than a role model that leads us on that career path? In an attempt to understand the human psyche, Carl Jung felt that we are guided by energy influences which he termed *archetypes*. In Jung's opinion an archetype is a universal symbol which seems to have an influence on a specific group of people. For instance, those who enter the medical profession may be guided by the healer archetype; those who pursue a career in teaching are guided by the teacher archetype.

An archetype is not necessarily a lifelong influence. People are known to be influenced by various factors in the life cycle which may be explained by the shift in archetypal energy. Just as a college student may change majors several times, or a person may change careers several times in a lifetime, archetypes can also change.

Archetypes are often expressed in various symbols or icons. A cross, an animal, a house, and a mother are all examples of archetypal symbols. We are often drawn to various symbols which communicate a specific archetypal energy that influences us. Jung said that archetypes are not instinctual. Rather they offer wisdom from the collective unconscious to gently guide us on the human path.

1. If you were to venture a guess, what archetype would you say you are most influenced by? If you are not sure, ask yourself what interests you most with regard to your life mission.

2. Archetypes are often represented in symbolic form. These symbols appear in jewelry, posters, T-shirts, and so forth. Are you drawn to any specific symbols? If so, which ones? What symbols are contained in the jewelry you wear? What attracted you to these symbols?

3. Archetypes may also manifest in dream symbols. Are there any messages from your dreams which may be best recognized as archetypes?

54

TIME AND MONEY

It has been said that two of the biggest constraints to leisure are time and money, or the lack thereof. It is no coincidence that these two factors are also two of the leading causes of stress. It is highly unlikely that a check for a million dollars in your mailbox tomorrow would solve your lifelong financial concerns. Neither would an extra hour in the day or an extra day in the week give you more time to get your work done. We are creatures of habit, and chances are that if we had more time and money, we would spend them much as we did before.

While we may not receive a million dollars or have extra hours in the day, we do have several resources to help us budget these constraints. In the information age of high technology, we are bombarded with interruptions. Time management isn't a luxury; it is a necessity. The keys to good time management include learning to prioritize responsibilities, to organize resources, to edit the unessentials, to set and evaluate goals, and to reward yourself for accomplishments.

Managing money is a different story. It involves separating your wants from your needs, keeping track of income and expenses, and living within your means—not the means of others, as in "keeping up with the Joneses." Money management means being disciplined. It means learning to enjoy delayed gratification. It also means finding and enjoying the things in life that are free.

Are time and money, or the lack of each, stressors for you? What is one thing you could start doing right now to manage your time better? Do you have champagne taste on a beer budget? What are some ways that you could gain a better handle on these two constraints to have more leisure and less stress?

55

POETRY IN MOTION

Yesterday is but a dream, tomorrow is only a vision,
But today well lived makes every yesterday a dream of happiness,
and every tomorrow a vision of hope.
Look well, therefore, to this day.
Ancient Sanscrit Proverb

Prose is not the only style thought to be therapeutic for journal entries. Poetry is also strongly recommended as a proven means to evoke an emotional catharsis. Although not all poems employ the elements of rhythm and rhyme, their use in writing poetry allows the author the chance to make order out of chaos, thus giving a feeling or sense of control with perceptions of stressful events. In addition, the poetic license to use metaphors and similes from personal feelings allows a deeper sense of emotional expression. Many poets, from Emily Dickinson and Robert Frost to Rod McEuen, have credited the use of poetry in their ability to gain a better perspective on expressing their feelings.

The healing process of self-expression through poetry, as described by M. R. Morrison in his book *Poetry as Therapy*, incorporates imagination, intuition, and the development of personal insight, three characteristics essential in the healing process. In turn, these poem entries augment self-awareness as the poem is first written and subsequently read in its entirety. As with other journal entries, poems can address a whole host of issues and emotions. For this reason poetry therapy is currently used as a therapeutic tool in the treatment of emotional disorders and illness, from hospitals to prisons. This writing method is encouraged as a complementary journal writing style. In the words of one anonymous philosopher, "Poetry is mass confusion understood."

Here's a chance to try your hand at poetry. Write a poem to express how you feel now. Perhaps the theme of your poem can be related to your life in general, or some specific aspect that seems to lie heavy on your mind (e.g., relationships, nature, holidays, anger, fear, or love). Remember, poems don't have to rhyme. You can write your poem any way you choose and about anything. Take a pen or pencil in hand and try to make some written order out of confusion that may harness your thoughts. You may be quite surprised at the results.

56

WHEN YOUR BIOGRAPHY BECOMES YOUR BIOLOGY

The cause of illness is ultimately connected to the inner stresses present in a person's life.
Carolyn Myss

In the early 1980s Robert Ader coined the term *psychoneuroimmunology* to designate a new field of study: mind-body medicine. What he and now countless others have discovered is that there is an amazing and profound connection between the mind and the body. Contrary to the opinion of French philosopher René Descartes, the mind and body are not separate entities. This means that our thoughts and feelings have an incredible impact on our physiology.

One person to emerge onto the stage of mind-body medicine is Carolyn Myss. A woman with an incredible ability to see what most others cannot, Myss has the gift to be able to look into a person's energy field and assist physicians to determine a disease or the cause of a disease. Myss has a remarkable rate of accuracy, especially considering that she can do this from hundreds of miles away. First intrigued by the concepts of the human energy field and the chakras (spinning wheels of energy positioned over several major body organs from head to spine), Myss has focused her own energy into teaching people about the awareness of mind-body-spirit harmony.

In her most recent book, *The Creation of Health*, Myss discusses the idea that a life history, in terms of experiences, becomes intertwined with the cells of a body. From hundreds of documented case studies she has come to the understanding that symptoms of disease and illness don't start in the body; they end there. Can cervical cancer be rooted in sexual molestation? Can lower back pain be rooted in financial insecurities? Myss thinks so. Judging by her track record (95 percent accuracy), she stands on pretty solid ground.

According to Carolyn Myss, getting your life story expressed and examined is important for optimal health. By coming to terms with your biography, you can release the negative energies that distort the integrity of every cell in your body. So what is your biography? What are some of the events that you now carry in the memories of each cell? Take some time to explore these and perhaps other life-long memories that may now be a part of your biology.

57

NO REGRETS

Tomorrow doesn't matter, for I have lived today.
Horace

How many times have you looked back on something you did or said and thought to yourself, "Gee, if only I had..." or "I should have..."? As the saying goes, "Hindsight is twenty-twenty!" Yet, for every action or behavior that we wish we had done differently, there are literally hundreds, if not thousands, of personal accomplishments we pass over as simple achievements or "things to be expected." Only when we look at this critical mass of lifelong experience do we realize that every experience, good or bad, is valuable if we take the time to learn from it.

Rather than dwelling on the "should haves," which can result in unnecessary guilt trips, take a moment to look back on the things that you have done that make you proud, happy, or just plain amazed. Recall those experiences that, if you had to live over again, you would do exactly the same way with no regrets whatsoever! Make a list of these memorable moments and jot down beside each what it was (the key factor) that made this episode memorable.

Many people on their deathbed look back on their lives and sigh as they recite a litany of regrets: things never accomplished and issues never resolved. Here is an inspirational message, attributed to Nadine Starr:

> If I had to do it over again, I would try to make more mistakes next time. I would relax. I would be sillier this trip. I would climb more mountains, swim more rivers, and watch more sunsets. If I had to do it over again, I would go places, do things, and travel lighter than I have. If I had my life to live over again, I would start barefoot in the spring and stay that way later in the fall. I would play hooky more. I would pick more daisies.

If you were to jump into the future for a moment and look back on your life, what events, what situations, and what experiences would you like to look back on as having done to complete satisfaction? Now, having pondered this and having made a list of these things, pick one or two—perhaps even three—and plan to do each one without a trace of regret. Remember one thing: Balance the freedom of choice with the responsibility of actions so you have no regrets! Every now and then, return to this list and add to it if necessary. Remember, every day is a new beginning; carpe diem—seize the day!

58
WHAT DID YOU SAY?

One might say that conversational skills don't belong in a stress management book, but nothing could be further from the truth. We are engaged in conversation from the moment we wake until the second we lay down our heads and enter the world of dreams. Whether it be with family, friends, customers, clients, peers, colleagues, strangers, or even voices on the radio and television, our minds are programmed to listen and respond to conversation virtually every minute of the day.

An old proverb states, "The three most important words to a successful relationship are *communication, communication, communication.*" It's true! As social animals we gravitate toward others to engage in conversation. Good communication skills are essential to every aspect of our lives. The elements of conversation are rather complicated because we communicate with more than just words and voices. In fact, more of our communication skills are nonverbal than verbal.

1. How good are your communication skills, both verbal and nonverbal? Are you aware of the messages you give to others with your clothing and hair styles, eye movements, posture, hand gestures, and facial expressions?

2. What is your body's silent message—that is, what is it saying without dialogue? Why? Is this the message you wish to convey?

3. Listening skills are as important as the ability to articulate your thoughts and feelings. Yet most people hear but seldom listen. More often than not, they begin to prepare what they are going to say within seconds of someone's beginning to speak or respond. How are your listening skills? What could you do to improve them?

4. Much research now suggests that men and women have different styles of communication. Have you ever noticed this? For example, have you noticed that when a woman says she'll call you tomorrow, she calls you tomorrow, whereas when a man says he'll call you tomorrow, most likely he will call you in a few days to a week?

5. Sometimes when we speak we are very indirect, not really saying what we mean. We beat around the bush. Do you find your verbal style is more indirect than direct? Do you tend to give mixed messages? After giving this some thought, can you think of ways to improve your verbal communication skills? Do you need to revise your nonverbal messages? How can you do this?

59

THE MEANING OF LIFE

We had to teach disparaging men and we had to remind ourselves that
it did not matter what we expected from life, rather what life expected from us.
Viktor Frankl, Nazi concentration camp survivor

"What is our purpose in life?" is by far the most important question we can ask. Finding the meaning of life is discovering the cornerstone of spiritual wellness. So often though, we journey through life looking to see what we can get out of our parents, our education, our job, and our government. Perhaps we have it all wrong! It's not what we can get out of life, it's what we give to life that makes it worth living. It is this perspective that inspired President Kennedy to create the Peace Corps. It also inspired him to say, "Ask not what your country can do for you. Ask what you can do for your country."

The college years are a good time to ask "What am I doing with my life?" This question often occurs when you're pondering what major to select or when you realize after graduation that you're in the wrong field. Trying to define your purpose in life is searching the depths of your soul. And it is a task that must be done frequently.

In your heart, what do you feel your purpose in life is? Why do you feel this way? And if you are at a point where you know the answer and you can articulate it, the next important question is: What is the best way to fulfill your life purpose so that it is meaningful and a significant contribution to humanity?

60

GUILT AND WORRY

The difference between a state of stress and a state of relaxation is simple. In a stressful frame of mind, we are preoccupied with events or issues from the past and/or the future. In a state of relaxation we can enjoy the present moment; we can absorb and appreciate life's simple pleasures. Stress robs us of the present moment.

As psychologist Wayne Dyer suggests in his best-selling book *Your Erroneous Zones*, two human emotions are employed exclusively in the stressful state of mind: guilt and worry. *Guilt* preoccupies the mind with events and feelings from the past, while *worry* attracts our attention to anticipated events. What both of these emotional states, or zones, have in common is that they both immobilize our thought processes and leave us unable to function at our best. These emotions cloud the mind and freeze rational thought processes that are truly needed to deal with our stressors.

While events from our past may serve as excellent learning experiences, all the guilt in the world will not change what has already occurred. Likewise, worrying is unproductive thinking. Too much of it can wreak havoc with the body's internal organs. Worrying about the future (not to be confused with planning for the future) is an unproductive emotion. Worrying is an immobilizing emotion. It wastes a lot of time, and time is too valuable a resource to waste. Most if not all of our stressors produce an excess of either one or both of these emotions. Not only do they rob us of the ability to enjoy the present moment, but they also inhibit us from acting in a way to resolve the issue that created these emotional responses.

Are you a chronic worrier? Are there specific items that you fret about, or do general concerns trigger your worries? Make a list of your top ten stressors again. Take a good look at them. Do they promote guilt or worry? Many people feel uncomfortable in the present moment. They would rather focus their attention on past or future events to avoid the present moment. Are you one of these people? Self-imposed guilt trips are very stressful. Is this an occasional characteristic of yours? Do you lay an occasional guilt trip on others to manipulate their emotions and behavior? If so, why? What are some ways to cut down on the use of these two emotions in your strategy to deal effectively with stress?

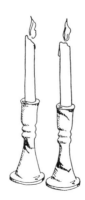

61

MY INNER RESOURCES

Be humble for you are made of earth.
Be noble for you are made of stars.
Serbian Proverb

If our collection of life experiences can be compared to that of a journey, then the problems, issues, difficulties, and dilemmas we encounter on that journey can likewise be compared to roadblocks on the human path.

When the traveler encounters a roadblock on a trail in the wilderness, the course of action to be taken depends on the tools and resources at hand. Obstacles can be climbed over, ducked under, skirted around, sawed through, blown up, or backed away from.

Obstacles we encounter on life's journey are neither fallen trees nor boulders. Nor can the experiential roadblocks we face be sawed through or blown up. In reality, these challenges come to us in the likes of alcoholic parents, financial debt, or the death of a spouse or close friend. In essence, they must be resolved and transcended. These are the only solutions.

Remember the story of Dorothy and the Wizard of Oz? This is a classic story of obstacles overcome by inner resources. Dorothy's goal was to return home; the roadblock on her journey was the witch. The scarecrow, tin man, and lion were personifications of her inner resources: intellect, compassion, and courage, respectively.

Consider inner resources for a moment. Comprised of traits that help us get through the tough times in our lives, they assist us to resolve and transcend whatever has been put in front of us and lend integrity to our human spirits. Humor, creativity, passion, willpower, courage, and faith are examples of special qualities that we can and often do use in troubled times. Let's take a look at your inner resources.

1. What obstacles are you facing right now in this leg of your human journey? Rather than just list them, take some time to flesh out the details of each one.

2. We all have inner resources, but not all us of make use of the same ones. Whether you call these talents, gifts, or special abilities, list your inner resources that help you dismantle and overcome the roadblocks you listed above. Are there any you feel are missing that would help you on your journey?

3. Inner resources can be compared to muscles. And like muscles, they atrophy with disuse or increase in size with some resistance. Now is the time to ask yourself which of your inner resources you have allowed to atrophy to a point where they are no longer functional. Next ask yourself, "What can I do to regain and strengthen these inner resources?"

62

MOTHER EARTH

Let us think of Mother Earth.
Native American prayer

It is no overstatement to say that the planet earth is in trouble! It is sick and desperately fighting for its survival. Water and air pollution, nuclear waste dumps, holes in the ozone, deforestation, and the incredible rate of extinction of plants and animals per day; the telltale signs are everywhere. All you need to do is listen to the news or read a magazine, and these stories jump out and smack you across the face.

It may seem hard to believe that the earth is a living entity. Western thought, so heavily grounded in the scientific ideology, makes this idea seem pagan at best. But, if you were to listen to the Wisdom Keepers of the earth's indigenous tribes, you would find that this notion of the earth as a living entity is not foolish or ludicrous. It is a simple truth. Even the ancient Greeks believed this, naming Mother Earth *Gaia*. Humans, once so close to the energies of the earth, have now grown very distant and separate from them. From air conditioned bedrooms (carbofluorocarbons) to the automobile (carbon monoxide), we have become slaves to the benefits of technology. Still, it is not uncommon to hear people say that technology can fix what technology has damaged—in essence-putting human capabilities above the powers of the earth and sky. In the profound words of Chief Seattle, "All things connect. Man did not weave the web of life, he is merely a strand in it. Whatever he does to the web, he does to himself."

Sometimes in the cyclone of daily hassles and catastrophic events of our lives, we become disconnected from the natural elements that surround us. Whether or not we realize it, like a web, we are strongly connected to the earth. Despite all the wonderful advances in technology, we are still very dependent on the fruits and sustenance that Mother Earth provides and the cycles in which she turns. *Stress* has recently been defined as being separated or disconnected from our friends, family, or the earth that sustains us. Inner peace is synonymous with connection and harmony with all. Therefore, part of the strategy to reduce stress is to reconnect with the planet we call home. Perhaps it's true that we can't change the world, but we can change a part of it by our interaction with it. This idea is summed up quite nicely in the slogan "Think globally, act locally."

Now is the time to do some soul-searching with your Mother Earth in mind. If this concept is something you have never given serious thought to, now is the time to get serious, and not in a stressful way either. Here are some questions you can ask yourself to get the ball rolling:

1. How would you best describe your relationship with the planet earth?

2. Do you see the earth as a rock spinning in space, or as a living entity that provides sustenance in one form or another to all her species of flora and fauna?

3. Getting back to nature can take many forms, from gardening to exotic vacations. What do you do to get back to nature when the urge strikes?

4. Biological rhythms and circadian variations are constant reminders that the earth strongly influences us. Are you in touch with these rhythms and, if not, why not?

5. Any good relationship takes work. If so inclined, what steps do you feel you can take to enhance your relationship with Mother Earth?

63

FROM A DISTANCE

Sometimes when we distance ourselves from our problems, we get a different and perhaps more objective viewpoint of our perceptions. Looking at ourselves through someone else's eyes gives us a chance to detach from our emotions long enough to find a new way to deal with the problem. When people write journal entries, they write almost exclusively in the first person (*I*). This first person viewpoint is often what separates autobiographical truth from a third person point of view, which is often incomplete because it lacks significant personal insight. But let us assume for a moment that an occasional journal entry could be written in the third person voice (*she, he*). Imagine what could be revealed using that unique insight that only you could provide, but with the objectivity of a third person with no emotional attachment—the best of both worlds.

A journal entry of this nature would read like a story or screenplay. It would have a plot (your stressor of the day), it would have character development (your thoughts and feelings this observer described), it would have mystery (how to resolve the stressor), and it might even have adventure and romance, but let's not get carried away. Save this journal entry for when you have had a really bad day or your mind has been weighed down so heavily that you just cannot be objective with your thoughts; then pull out a pen and write about this concern from the perspective of someone else looking at the situation. You'll be surprised at just how therapeutic and revealing this type of entry can be.

64

BEHAVIORS I'D LIKE TO CHANGE

If one desires change, one must be that change first
before that change can take place.
Gita Bellin

If you are like most people, you seek some type of self-improvement on a regular basis. Perhaps it's to correct something you notice yourself doing. More likely, it may be a response to a friendly suggestion from a friend, or worse, someone you aren't particularly fond of. The most recognized time to make behavioral changes is January 1, when the year is new, the slate is clean, and the winds of change are in the air. Another time that we are reminded to make changes is on or around our birthday—again a clean slate.

Two types of personalities and the respective behaviors linked with stress have now become household words: Type A and Codependent. Type A behaviors include compulsive actions related to time urgency, super-competitiveness, and hostile aggression. These characteristics, primarily feelings of unresolved hostility, are thought to be closely associated with coronary heart disease. Codependent behaviors include perfectionism, super over-achievement, ardent approval seeking, control of others, inability to express anger and other feelings, ardent loyalty to loved ones, and overreacting. These types of behavior are now strongly linked to cancer.

Sometimes we are aware of our behaviors, but many times we are not. Specific actions can become so ingrained in our being that they become second nature and we seldom consider them. It is only at those times when something we do is pointed out to us, or in an unguarded moment, that we see ourselves as perhaps others see us.

Behavioral psychologists have come to agree that changes are made first through awareness and then through motivation to change. But changing several habits at one time, which people usually try to do at the start of each new year, is very difficult, if not impossible. What is now commonly suggested is to try to change one behavior at a time. This way there is a greater chance of accomplishment. There is a progression of steps that, when taken, augments this behavior cheange process.

1. Become aware of eyour current behavior (i.e., biting your fingernails).

2. Think of a new mind frame to precede the new behavior you want to introduce (biting my nails is bad, and I need to stop doing this).

3. Substitute a new and more desirable behavior in place of the old one (in the act of biting nails, stop and take a few deep breaths to relax).

4. Reevaluate the outcome of trying the new behavior and see what you think (conscious breathing helped, especially on that date last night; let's keep trying this).

Sometimes it helps to write it down. Do you have any behaviors that you wish to modify or change? What are your options? Sketch them out here!

65

SWEET FORGIVENESS

You cannot shake hands with a clenched fist.
Indira Ghandi

Every act of forgiveness is an act of unconditional love. If unresolved anger is a toxin to the spirit, forgiveness is the antidote, and where anger is a roadblock, forgiveness is a ladder to climb above and transcend the experience. For forgiveness to be complete and unconditional, you must be willing to let go of all feelings of anger, resentment, and animosity. Sweet forgiveness cannot hold any taste of bitterness as they are mutually exclusive. Victimization is a common feeling when one encounters stressors in the form of another person's behaviors. When we sense that our human rights have been violated, feelings of rage can quickly turn into feelings of resentment. Left unresolved, these toxic thoughts can taint the way we treat others and ourselves. To forgive those who we feel have wronged us is not an easy task. Often it's a process, and at times, a very long process at that. Yet turning the other cheek does not mean you have to let people walk all over you. Forgiveness is not a surrender of your self-esteem, nor is it a compromise of your integrity. When you can truly forgive the behavior of those whom you feel violated by, you let go of the feelings of control and become free to move on with your life. Resentment and grudges can become roadblocks on the human path. Forgiveness turns a hardened heart into an open passageway to progress on life's journey. Think for a moment of someone who might have violated your humanness. Is it time to let go of some toxic thoughts and initiate a sense of forgiveness?

To begin this journal entry, write the name of that person or those persons toward whom you feel some level of resentment. Beside each name write down what action or behavior it was that offended you and why you feel so violated. What feelings arise in you when you see this person, or even hear his or her name. Next, make a note of how long you have felt this way toward this person. Finally, search your soul for a way to forgive the people on your list, even if it means just to acknowledge their human spirit. Then practice the act of forgiveness as best you can, and let the feelings of resentment go.

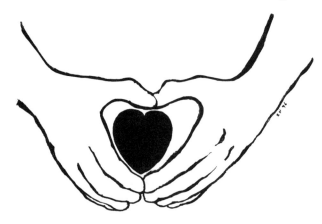

130

66

LOVE

Love means letting go of fear.
Gerald Jampolski

Love. It seems that no other concept has puzzled humankind so much as this single word. It is love that gives life and paradoxically people lose their lives in its name. As a professor who studied, taught, and has written several books on the subject, Leo Buscaglia admits that to define love is virtually impossible. Impossible it may be, but people continue to try to describe this abstract term as they best know how. Among authors, poets, songwriters, and actors, the vehicles of love's message are endless.

After years of research, Buscaglia offered his own incomplete definition, suggesting that love is that which brings you back to your real self. In Buscaglia's book entitled *LOVE*, he writes, "For love and the self are one, and the discovery of either is the realization of both." Just as charity is said to begin at home, so too must love reside within the individual before it can be shared. Buscaglia suggests that to share love, you must first give yourself permission to possess and nurture this quality toward yourself. Furthermore, self-love begins with self-acceptance, unconditional self-acceptance.

It is interesting to note that the psychology field has pretty much ignored this emotion during the twentieth century, instead giving the limelight to anxiety and fear. Because of sexual connotations, love as an inner resource has been virtually disregarded, much to the detriment of all human society. More recently, through the work of Buscaglia, Kubler-Ross, Siegel, Borysenko and others, this aspect of the human condition is being given more serious attention. In the much acclaimed book *The Road Less Traveled*, psychiatrist M. S. Peck offers his own insights about the concept of love. From empirical observations, Peck perceives that there are many echelons of love: sharing, caring, trust, passion, and compassion, with the highest level of love being a divine essence he calls *grace*.

Let there be no doubt, love is a profound concept. It is a value, an emotion, a virtue, a spiritual essence, an energy, and, to many people, an enigma. Love can inflict emotional pain just as it can heal the scars and bruises of the soul. It can make a fool out of the bravest man and a hero out of an underdog. The expression of love can be quite intimidating as well, and in American society love is often extended with conditions. Ultimately, it is these strings that taint our perception of love, whereas unconditional love may be the ultimate expression of grace. The word *love* often brings to mind visions of Hollywood silver screen passion. We have been socialized to think that love has to be as dynamic as Superman, yet the power of love can be as subtle as a smile or a happy thought.

If you were to attempt to define love, how would you begin your interpretation of this concept? Is your expression of love limited by your level of self–acceptance? When you express your love to others, do you find that you attach conditions with it? In your opinion, how does falling in love differ from feeling unconditional love? Add any thoughts to your definition of love here as well.

67

MY BODY'S RHYTHMS

The body has an internal clock that runs on a 24- to 25-hour day. If you were to lock yourself away from all the natural elements (sunlight, temperature fluctuations, etc.) and the grips of technology (e.g., TVs, radios, and computers), as some people have for research purposes, you would find that your body falls into a natural rhythm.

This natural rhythm is called a *circadian rhythm*—based on a 24+ hour day, and to a large extent, this rhythm is based on and is strongly influenced by the elements of the natural world: the earth's rotation, the gravitational pull, the earth's axis and several other influences we are probably not even aware of.

There are other types of rhythms that influence our body as well: *infradian rhythms* (less than 24-hour cycles), such as rapid eye movement cycles and stomach contractions caused by hunger; and *ultradian rhythms* (more than 24-hour cycles), such as menstrual periods and red blood cell formation.

It has been said that as we continue to embrace the achievements of high technology and separate ourselves even further from the reaches of nature we throw off our body's rhythms. When these rhythms are thrown off for too long, we begin to see various organs that are dependent on the regularity of these rhythms go into a state of dysfunction.

A rushed life (e.g., college life) is not structured with a particular order for body rhythms. You can eat dinner one day at 6:00 p.m. and the next day at 9:30 p.m. We won't even talk about sleep! Perhaps at a young age your body can rebound from these cyclical misgivings. More likely than not though, regular disruptions in the body's rhythms will manifest quickly in various ways, like irritability, fatigue, lack of hunger, restless sleep, and insomnia.

1. What is your general sense of your body's rhythms?

2. Do you keep to a regular schedule with regard to eating, sleeping, and exercise, or does your time for these vary from day to day?

3. If you are a female, how regular are your menstrual periods? Can you identify a pattern with your nutritional habits, stress levels, and other daily rituals that may influence your menses?

4. How closely are you connected with nature? Do you spend time outdoors every day? Do you find yourself more tired, perhaps even more irritable, as we shift from fall into winter?

68

LESSONS LEARNED

Is it possible that life is one big schoolroom or that the planet Earth is a laboratory for learning? There are many people who believe so. But unlike the structural classrooms that we attend from kindergarten through graduate school, the classroom of life is virtually experimental in nature. Moreover, there are neither grades nor curves. There are no diplomas, just a wealth of accumulated knowledge that we call *wisdom*.

The school of life does not require studying in the form of memorization as much as it necessitates a continual synthesis of information and our experiences. The goal of our individual lesson plans is to discover the universal truths and to apply these in the framework of our lives. Each experience has a lesson to offer if we choose to take the time to learn from it. As with other forms of schooling, there are times when we play hooky and miss out on important material. In the end, our lives are an open book in which we write the lessons we've learned.

Some of life's lessons are so obvious that we walk right through, missing them completely. Others are so painful that we choose to avoid them. However, through it all we are very much aware, either consciously or unconsciously, of the meaning of our experiences. An ancient Chinese proverb states, "When the pupil is ready, the teacher will come," meaning that when we take the time to explore the purpose of our life experiences, we will understand, and the lessons will be learned. To be "ready" is to be still with thought, allowing the mind liberty to interpret the meaning of these lessons.

Before you start this journal theme, you might want to sit comfortably, close your eyes for a moment, and relax. Take a few deep breaths and begin to clear your mind of any distracting thoughts. Then use the following questions to ready the student within yourself so that the teacher may come.

1. What would you say is the most valuable of all the lessons that you have learned in your life to date?

2. What events led to this experience?

3. What was it that sparked this moment of revelation?

4. Are there any experiences that you still question the meaning of?

5. What events that have caused you pain and that you are avoiding may ultimately bear the fruit of understanding once resolved?

6. Finally, there is an expression that says, "To know and not to do is not to know." Are there some lessons you thought ou had learned and then forgot to apply in your life that caused history to repeat itself? If so, what are they? Do you have any other comments you wish to add?

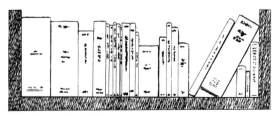

69

THE HOLOGRAPHIC UNIVERSE

As long as the formless and breathtaking freedom of the beyond remains frightening to us we will continue to dream a hologram for ourselves that is comfortably solid and well defined.
Michael Talbot

Scientists spend lifetimes theorizing about the dynamics of the universe and the nature of reality. The *mechanistic theory* compares the operation of the universe to that of a big grandfather clock, with almost everything rationally and predictably explained by cause and effect. The *chaos theory* says that the universe is multilayered and dimensional, and that what appears to be chaos is really just a lower form of order. The *theory of implicate order* holds that everything is connected. The *holographic theory* states that the whole is contained in each part. Lately, this theory has taken on great importance regarding how we live our lives and how we deal with stress.

If you were to cut a holographic image in any number of pieces, each piece would contain the entire image. Several examples from other fields support the concept of the holographic theory: in acupuncture the entire meridian map can be found within the ear; reflexology is based on the premise that a map of the body can be found on the sole of the foot.

In his book *The Holographic Universe*, Michael Talbot expounds upon the holographic theory, saying that we are part of the whole but also contain the whole within us. The holographic theory suggests that at some level we are all connected and the answers to our problems are found in the wisdom within all of us.

If this is true, then we contain within us the strength of moving water and the stability of mountains. We contain all the resources needed to overcome all the obstacles we meet on life's journey. Ancient wisdom suggests that we are all connected. The holographic theory supports this premise. With this in mind, take a moment to reflect on the concept of connectedness, the holographic universe, and how this may assist you in your human endeavors.

70

SELF-ESTEEM
THE BOTTOM LINE

No one can make you feel inferior without your consent.
Eleanor Roosevelt

Many themes in this journal workbook revolve around the concept of self-esteem. Self-esteem is considered by many to be the bottom line with regard to the perceptions of stressors and, indeed, how we manage our stress. *Self-esteem* is often defined as our personal level of self-approval. It is used synonymously with self-worth and self-respect. Ultimately, strong self-esteem equates to the degree of acceptance and love we bestow upon ourselves. High self-esteem can sometimes be confused with over-confidence, cockiness, and aggressiveness. So we tend to compensate by acting humble. Often, the result is self-depreciation to the point of negativism, and negativism perpetuates low self-esteem. Today, society gives many mixed messages which value both humility and assertiveness. It's a fine line drawn and straddled. We must learn to walk in balance.

Self-esteem is a complex concept. It includes, but is not limited to, self-understanding, acceptance, love, forgiveness, personal value system, and atonement. Self- esteem is as hard to measure as it is to define. Suffice to say that each of us is generally aware of where our self-esteem is as well as of daily fluctuations and things that inflate or deflate it . Most everything we say, think, feel, or do is a function of our self-esteem. In turn, messages that we communicate to ourselves and others from our thoughts, feelings, and actions can reinforce either low or high self-esteem. When our self-esteem is low, like the bull's eye of a target we become more susceptible to life's pressures. Conversely, when we are feeling good about ourselves, problems tend to roll off our backs quite easily. Stress becomes manageable or is simply dismissed altogether. There are four factors that contribute to strong self-esteem:

1. **Uniqueness:** Characteristics that make you feel special and unique.
2. **Power:** Feelings of self-reliance and self-efficacy, a "can do" attitude.
3. **Modeling:** Having a mentor or role model to serve as a guide on your own life journey.
4. **Connectiveness:** Feelings of bonding and belonging with others; your network of friends and support groups.

The self-esteem concept, referred to indirectly in previous journal themes, merits its own theme to write about. Take a moment to contemplate the idea of self-esteem, what your threshold is, and the bounds within which it oscillates. What are some ways to raise your threshold for a higher level of self-esteem? Do you see a relationship between your current self-esteem threshold and how well you deal with stress? Try to identify the following: five characteristics that make you unique, five factors that give you a sense of empowerment, five role models or mentors, and five friends or groups of people you consider to be part of your support system or connectedness.

71

THE POWER OF SUGGESTION

Have you ever heard of Neuro-Linguistic Programming (NLP)? It is a behavior modification program based on the concept that words have specific meanings that our unconscious minds pick up on, directs our actions, and ultimately, even our state of health.

To understand this concept it helps to understand that our conscious mind makes up only a small portion (10 percent) of our total mind. This means that our unconscious mind is really both the navigator and pilot when it comes to our actions and behaviors, yet the conscious mind can override the system at times and cause some problems, especially when thoughts are not congruent with those of the unconscious mind. It gets complicated, but suffice it to say that although the unconscious mind thinks in terms of metaphors and similes, it takes quite literally that which the conscious mind articulates, even when the conscious mind speaks figuratively.

Neuro-Linguistic Programming suggests that the power of words and expressions we use in everyday life can have a big impact on various aspects of our lives. For instance to say "That sports car is to die for" may carry with it a foreshadowing of a date with the Grim Reaper. To say that your boss is "a pain in the ass" may indeed foreshadow some lower back pain.

To go one step further, the unconscious mind may suggest a host of expressions that predict the direction of your health; for example, when you say something like "My skin is so sensitive to sunlight that I am a walking tumor waiting to happen."

Neuro-Linguistic Programming invites us to choose our words cautiously and to get in the practice of thinking before we speak. Remember, the power of suggestion is quite tremendous, especially when the suggestion comes from the depths of your own mind.

1. Take notice of the selection of words you use in everyday conversation. Make note of expressions, idioms, colloquialisms, and vernacular that have both a literal and figurative meaning.

2. How often do you use negatives when you speak? If you are like most people, you probably use them quite often. It is said that the unconscious mind doesn't understand negatives. Try converting the negatives to positives. For example, when you say, "I won't flunk this test," the unconscious mind translates this into "I will flunk this test." Jot down all of the negativisms you find yourself thinking or saying and then next to each, write down a positive expression to use instead. For example, you could say, "I will pass this test."

3. Take note of Freudian slips, or expressions that come out inadvertently when talking and reveal some deeper unconscious thoughts. Write these down as well, and study them.

72

HERE COMES THE JUDGE

*The problem with judgmental thinking is that
sometimes it channels our thinking in the wrong direction.*
Roger von Oech

To judge or not to judge, that is the question! We have an amazing ability to perceive the world around us. By and large, we perceive through our sense of judgment; that's good, this is bad, this is nice, that sucks, and so on. From an early age, one of the first thinking skills we access is pattern recognition, a type of judgment skill. From here we are taught to judge by what is deemed good or bad.

Judgment is considered to be a left-brain thinking skill. When combined with other left-brain functions such as analysis, linear thinking, rational thinking, and logical thinking, we tend to become left-brain dominant, focusing on problems. The eye of critical awareness can also be directed inward, making it hard to live up to our own expectations of perfection.

Judgment is not altogether bad. We need judgment skills to help us make decisions in times of stress—many of which may seem like life or death situations. But if we overuse this thinking skill, then we begin to force judgment on everything. As psychologist Abraham Maslow once said, "If your only tool is a hammer, you will see every problem as a nail."

1. Do you see yourself as a judgmental person? If so, why?

2. When do you think using your sense of judgment is stress-relieving rather than stress-producing?

3. As described above, left-brain dominant people tend to be more critical, judgmental, rational and logical, while right-brain dominant people tend to be more accepting, receptive, intuitive, and playful. The best scenario is to have a balance of both right- and left-brain skills. If you were to choose between right- and left-brain dominance, which would you say best described you? Why?

If you are not sure to what extent your mind thinks judgmentally, you may want to take the Myers-Briggs Inventory to see how strong this aspect of your thinking skills is.

73

WALKING IN BALANCE

Walk softly on the back of Mother Earth.
Hopi Saying

There is a native American expression used to explain the concept of living in harmony with nature. It says to always find yourself "walking in balance."

The term *walking in balance* also means to make the effort to achieve balance between mind, body, spirit and emotions. Having had some exposure to this concept and knowing that wellness is the integration, balance, and harmony of the mind, body, spirit, and emotions, what are several things you can do to enhance the aspects of integration, balance, and harmony? List twenty-five things that you either do or can include in your lifestyle to walk in balance.

1. _____

2. _____

3. _____

4. _____

5. _____

6. _____

7. _____

8. _____

9. _____

10. _____

11. _____

12. _____

13. _____

14. _____

15. _____

16. _____

17. _____

18. _____

19. _____

20. _____

21. _____

22. _____

23. _____

24. _____

25. _____

74

FRIENDS IN NEED

And let there be no purpose in friendship save the deepening of the spirit.
Kahlil Gibran

What is a friend? Perhaps it's someone to share precious moments of life with. Perhaps a friend is a person to confide our innermost thoughts and feelings to. Most likely a friend is someone just to be there at times when we are in need of a helping hand or a comforting hug. Friends are all this and more.

As human beings, we are social by nature. Although there are times when being alone can help us energize our souls, we need to balance these times with the interactions and exchanges with those people we feel closest to, our network of friends.

Some interesting findings have emerged from research investigating the health and longevity of the world's oldest living citizens. We now know that involvement with friends is as important to our health as regular exercise, proper nutrition, and sleep. When we are troubled, our friends can help buffer or neutralize the stress and tension that we feel. The bottom line is that the collection of friends we call our support group can serve as an effective means to cope with stress.

As we grow and mature, so our relationships with friends. The bonds we have with some people continually strengthen over time and distance, while others seem to fray or fade. We often attract people who share our interests and ambitions. In some cases, our closest friends can seem more like family than our brothers and sisters. In every case, friendships, like house plants and pets, need attention and nurturing. Every now and then it is a good idea to take a moment to evaluate our friendships, to see if they are truly fulfilling our needs. This inventory of friends can let us know if we have outgrown or grown apart from some people, and if so, why. It can also make us aware of the qualities that comprise a good, close, or best friend, and the differences between a good friend and an acquaintance. We also need to evaluate if we are making an equal contribution to each relationship. Here are some questions to help you with this assessment.

1. How would you best define the word *friend*, and what does being a friend mean to you?

2. What is it about you that draws a person into your life to become a friend?

3. Make a list of all your current friends. Are any members of your family in this group? How has this list changed over the past five years?

4. How would you evaluate your current circle of friends? Do you have several acquaintances that you call your friends?

5. Does your support group consist of people in different social circles, or is yours a closed circle of friends? Why would friends in different circles be of value?

6. What is it that keeps your bonds of friendships strong, and what is it that lets some friendships fade away?

7. Are there any additional comments you wish to add here?

75

HEALTH OF THE HUMAN SPIRIT

The health of the human spirit is wonderfully simple to achieve but difficult to maintain. Although there are endless ways to make your spirit soar, it is so easy to get caught up in the day-to-day nonsense that our spirits drag on the ground.

Aside from the processes of centering, emptying, grounding, and connecting, there are several recipes for nurturing the health of the human spirit. Here is a short list:

1. **The art of self-renewal:** finding and practicing new ways to re-energize ourselves and taking time alone to restore our sense of who we are.

2. **The practice of sacred rituals:** taking time to honor that part of ourselves and nature that comes from the divine essence of the universe.

3. **Embracing the shadow:** acknowledging the dark side of our personalities and learning to accept those parts of ourselves even if we don't like them.

4. **Acts of forgiveness:** learning to forgive ourselves and others who we feel may have violated our humanness; learning to let go without resentment or shame.

5. **Surrendering the ego:** continually dismantling the walls of the ego to connect with our higher selves.

6. **Compassion in action:** remembering that we are all connected and love is the bond that ties us together. Acts of compassion are for no other purpose than to share the expression of unconditional love.

7. **Living our joy:** living in the moment with the idea that there are a host of experiences that can bring a smile to the face and joy to the heart.

Reflecting on these seven ideas, address each one by commenting on how you engage in the health of your own spirit.

76

LIGHT AT THE END
OF THE TUNNEL

Doubt is a pain too lonely to know that faith is his twin brother.
Kahlil Gibran

There are times when it seems that our problems are so bad there is simply no way out. But no matter how bad our problems are, they are never as bad as we think. And no matter how intense our stressors are, there is always light at the end of the tunnel. This glimmer of light is faith. Faith! It is said to move mountains, part waters, and perform miracles. Faith is nothing less than our desire to fly, and nothing more than the wind beneath our wings.

Faith is not a belief in something outside ourselves that makes all our problems go away or answers our desperate prayers. Faith is a deep-seated conviction that all will be well. Enacting the inner resource of faith is accepting the realization that we are not alone on our human journey; in fact, we are part of a much bigger whole. Calling our faith into play is the realization of this divine connection. Faith is a hybrid of confidence, patience, compassion, optimism, and intuition. There is also a component of faith that is part mystery, for it simply cannot be explained in human terms. Scientists cannot measure it, nor should they even try.

One cannot address the concept of faith without talking about blind faith. Faith requires a little homework. Blind faith is a lazy person's approach to problems and in the long run will get you nowhere. So what is the required homework in the faith equation? In terms of stress management we call this information seeking, where as many facts are gathered as is humanly possible to gain the greatest understanding of the problem at hand. Blind faith is faith that hasn't done its homework. Putting our trust in a source greater than ourselves is neither a sign of helplessness nor naiveté. Does faith have limits? Perhaps! We must live our own lives; we cannot expect someone else to do it for us. Conversely, thinking that we can handle every problem on our own is naive. If we are going to rise above life's problems, there will be times when we will need to exercise our faith that everything will work out all right.

1. Overall, on a scale of 1–10 (with 10 being the highest) how would you rate your level of faith?

2. How does fear or anxiety affect your level of confidence in tough times?

3. Can you describe a time when faith delivered, when the forces of the universe came together for you to achieve your goal(s)? Please write about it here.

77

LETTING GO OF STRESS

Tension is who you think you should be.
Relaxation is who you are.
Ancient Chinese proverb

As humans, we may have evolved in many ways since the days of cave men and cave women, but by and large, we are still hunters and gatherers. Only in this day and age we don't just gather material possessions. We tend to hang on to various emotions, which over time become emotional baggage.

In the Eastern culture, there is a concept known as *detachment*. It means to let go of something—unconditionally. The thought behind this concept is that when we let go of our attachments, we become unencumbered. We set ourselves free. By letting go of those things which weigh us down we are free to travel light again. Detachment doesn't mean indifference, however. In other words, to let go of a thought or possession doesn't mean that we abandon compassion for the sake of freedom, nor do we act rude or indifferent.

Letting go of stress invites us to abandon emotions that are anchored in anger and fear. But detachment isn't always easy. Many people cling to these emotions and the problems related to them because they seem to validate our existence and stroke the ego. Letting go of stress is a way to cleanse oneself of the negativity generated by the ego and begin anew.

Is there something you are hanging on to—a sense of anger or fear that needs to be released? Are you currently attached to some feelings (and their corresponding behaviors or possessions) that might be better left behind? Explore the concept of detachment here.

78

REFLECTIONS
YOUR JOURNAL SUMMARY

Every now and then it is a good idea to look back and see where you have traveled. A reflection on the past often gives us insight into how best to deal with the future. This reflection is a personal historical perspective, highlighting patterns and behaviors of our lives, and as the saying goes, "Those who fail to learn history's lessons are bound to repeat them."

Often, we see our lives on a day-to-day basis. This is how the mind works best. However, like the study of history, we can learn much about ourselves by reviewing our past thoughts, attitudes, perceptions, and behaviors. Many times, patterns begin to emerge that are impossible to detect on a day-to-day basis. Patterns once discovered can either help us deal with our stressors or perpetuate our thought process, which in turn feeds the whole process of stress. By observing these patterns, our awareness increases, and we can plan strategies to make our lives a little easier.

Now it is time to review your journal and see what lessons there are to be learned from your travels. Reread your journal entries, particularly the days when you just wrote what was on your mind. Then look for patterns or habits that stand out—those that perhaps you didn't know were part of your personality. Then begin to summarize what you have learned about yourself from rereading your journal entries. Rereading journal entries is like looking at old photographs. Some shots may not be too flattering, while others are going to bring back some great memories. You may also wish to reflect on how rereading your thoughts and feelings might give you insight to help chart the next passage of your life journey until it comes time to reread it again. The questions to be asked from this summary are "What have I learned about myself from rereading these journal entries?" and "How can I use what have I learned to help me down the road as I travel onward ?"

REFERENCES

Allgeir, E., and Allgeir, A., *Sexual Interactions* (4th ed.). D. C. Heath, Lexington, MA, 1995.

Andreas, S., and Falkner (ed.), *NLP: The New Technology of Achievement*. Quill Books, New York, 1994.

Baum, L. F. *The Wizard of Oz*. Random House, New York, 1986.

Beattie, M., *Codependent No More*. Harper/Hazelton, New York, 1987.

———, *Beyond Codependency*. Harper/Hazelton, New York, 1989.

Black Elk, W., and Lyons, W., *Black Elk*. Harper, San Francisco, 1990.

Borysenko, J., *Minding the Body, Mending the Mind*. Bantam Books, New York,1984.

Boyd, D., *Rolling Thunder*. Delta, New York, 1974.

Branden, N., *The Six Pillars of Self-Esteem*. Bantam Books, New York, 1994.

Buscaglia, L., *LOVE*. Fawcett Crest, New York, 1972.

———, *Living, Loving & Learning*. Fawcett Books, New York, 1982.

Casey, K. and Vanceburg, M., *The Promise of a New Day*. HarperCollins, New York, 1983.

Dossey, L., *Healing Wounds: The Power of Prayer and the Practice of Medicine*. HarperCollins, New York, 1993.

Dyer, W., *Your Erroneous Zones*. Avon Books, New York, 1976.

Fanning, P., *Visualization for Change*. New Harbinger, Oakland, CA,1988.

Frankl, V., *Man's Search for Meaning*. Pocket Books, New York, 1984.

Gibran, K., *The Prophet*. Alfred A. Knopf, New York, 1981.

Hall, C., *A Primer of Freudian Psychology*. Mentor Books, New York, 1954.

Hayward, S., *A Guide for the Advanced Soul*. In-Tune Books, Avalon, Australia,1984.

Jampolski, G., *Love is Letting Go of Fear*. Celestial Arts, Berkeley, CA, 1979.

Jung, C. G., *Man and His Symbols*. Anchor Press, New York, 1964.

———, *Mandalas of Symbolism*. Princeton University Press, Princeton, NJ, 1973.

Klein, A., *The Healing Power of Humor*. J. P. Tarcher, Los Angeles, 1989.

Kübler-Ross, E., *Death, The Final Stage of Growth*. Touchstone, New York, 1987.

Lerner, H., *The Dance of Anger*. Harper and Row, New York, 1985.

Lindbergh, A. M., *Gift from the Sea*. Vintage Books, New York, 1978.

Maltz, M., *Psycho-Cybernetics*. Pocket Books, New York, 1960.

Martz, H., *If I Had to Live my Life Over Again, I Would Pick More Daisies*. Papier-Mache Press, Watsonville, CA, 1993.

Maslow, A. *The Farther Reaches of Human Nature*. Penguin Books, New York, 1971.

McGaa, E. (Eagleman), *Mother Earth Spirituality*. HarperCollins, San Francisco, 1990.

Moore, T., *Care of the Soul*. Harper Perennial, New York, 1992.

Ornstein, N., and Sobel, D., *Healthy Pleasures*. Addison-Wesley, Reading, MA, 1990.

Peck, M. S., *The Road Less Traveled*. Touchstone, New York, 1978.

———, *The Different Drum*. Touchstone, New York, 1987.

Peter, L., and Dana, B., *The Laughter Prescription*. Ballantine, New York, 1982.

Roberts, E., and Amidon, E., *Earth Prayers from Around the World*. HarperCollins, San Francisco, 1991.

Rotter, J., Generalized expectancies for internal versus external control reinforcement, *Psychological Monographs*, 609: 80, 1966.

Sams, J., *Earth Medicine*. HarperCollins, San Francisco, 1994.

Sanford, J., *Dreams and Healing*. Paulist Press, New York, 1978.

Seattle, Chief, A letter from Chief Seattle, 1855 (from Ed McGaa), *Mother Earth Spirituality*. HarperCollins, San Francisco, 1990.

Schaef, A.W., *Co-Dependence: Misunderstood, Mistreated*. Harper and Row, New York, 1986.

Shealy, N., and Myss, C., *The Creation of Health: The Emotional, Psychological and Spiritual Responses That Promote Health and Healing*. Stillpoint, Walpole, NH, 1988.

Siegel, B., *Love, Medicine, & Miracles*. Perennial, New York, 1987.

———, *Peace, Love, & Healing*. Perennial, New York, 1990.

Simonton, O. C., Simonton, S., and Creighton, J., *Getting Well Again*. Bantam Books, New York, 1978.

Sperry, R., The great cerebral commisure, *Scientific American*, 44-52, 1964.

Tannen, D., *That's Not What I Meant! How Conversational Style Makes or Breaks Relationships*. Ballantine, New York, 1986.

———, *You Just Don't Understand: Women and Men in Conversation*. Ballantine, New York, 1990.

von Oech, R., *A Whack on the Side of the Head*. Warner Books, New York, 1983.

———, *A Kick in the Seat of the Pants*. Perennial, New York, 1986.

Weisinger, H., *The Anger Workout Book*, Quill Books, Harlinton, TX, 1985.

Yogananda, P., *Inner Reflections*. Self-Realization Fellowship, Los Angeles, 1996.

JOURNAL WRITING
ADDITIONAL RESOURCES

Abbott, H. P., *Diary Fiction: Writing as Action*. Cornell University Press, New York, 1984.

Abercrombie, B., *Keeping a Journal*. Margaret K. McKelderry Books, New York, 1987.

Adams, K., *Journal to the Self*. Warner Books, New York, 1990.

Baldwin, C., *One to One: Self-Understanding through Journal Writing*. M. Evans & Co., New York, 1977.

Britton, J., Burgess, T., Martin, N., McLeod, A., and Rosen, H., *The Development of Writing Abilities*. Macmillan, London, 1975.

Buzan, T., *Use Both Sides of Your Brain*. E. P. Dutton, New York, 1983.

Capacchione, L., *The Creative Journal: The Art of Finding Yourself*. Swallow Press. Athens, GA,1979.

DeVoto, B. (ed.), *The Journals of Lewis and Clark*. Houghton Mifflin, Boston, 1953.

Dinesen, I., *Out of Africa*. Random House, New York, 1983.

Foster, S., with Little, M., *The Book of the Vision Quest; Personal Transformations in the Wilderness*. Prentice–Hall, New York, 1988.

Fulwiler, T. (ed.), *Journals Across the Disciplines*. Northeast Regional Exchange, Chelmsford, MA, 1985.

Goldberg, N., *Writing Down the Bones*. Shambhala, Boston, 1986.

Hagan, K. L., *Internal Affairs: A Journal Keeping Workbook for Self-Intimacy*. Escapadia Press, Atlanta, 1988.

Holly, M. L., *Writing to Grow: Keeping a Personal/Profession Journal*. Heinemann, Portsmouth, 1989.

Kaiser, R. B., The way of the journal, *Psychology Today*, 15:64–65, 1981.

Leedy, J. L., *Poetry Therapy: The Use of Poetry in the Treatment of Emotional Disorders*. J. B. Lippincott, Philadelphia, 1969.

Mallon, T., *A Book of One's Own: People and Their Diaries*. Ticknor and Fields, New York, 1984.

Mayer, H., Lester, N., and Pradl, G., *Learning to Write, Writing to Learn*. Boynton/Cook, Portsmouth, NH, 1983.

Morrison, M. R., *Poetry as Therapy*. Human Sciences Press, New York, 1987.

Pennebaker, J. W., *Opening Up: The Healing Power of Confiding in Others*. William Morrow, New York, 1990.

Progoff, I., *At a Journal Workshop*. Dialogue House Library, New York, 1975.

———, *The Practice of Process Meditation*. Dialogue House Library, New York, 1980.

Rainer, T., *The New Diary*. J. P. Tarcher, Los Angeles, 1978.

Rico, G. L., *Writing the Natural Way*. J. P. Tarcher, Los Angeles, 1983.

Seaward, B. L., *Managing Stress: Principles and Strategies for Health and Wellbeing*. Jones and Bartlett, Boston, MA, 1994.

Simons, G. F., *Keeping Your Personal Journal*. Ballantine/Epiphany, New York, 1978.

ADDITIONAL JOURNAL ENTRIES